Food

Culture

Shopping

Going out

Gardens

Beach

Activities

Excursions

A to Z of Tips for Visitors

Editor: Julia Kaufhold
Text, research & photos: Julia Kaufhold
Translation: Will Sleath, St Ives
Illustrations & maps: Nicola Clark, St Ives
Layout & typesetting: TypoWerkstatt Timon Schlichenmaier, Hamburg
Printing & binding: Druckerei Jagusch GmbH, Wallenfels/Germany

All information in this book has been collected by the author, is correct to the best of her
knowledge and has been carefully checked by the publisher, but incorrect content cannot
be totally excluded. The publisher thus emphasises that all information is without gua-
rantee in terms of product liability, and that no responsibility or liability can be assumed
for any inconsistencies. Comments about quality are the purely subjective opinion of the
author and are not intended as publicity for companies and products. We request your
understanding in this matter, and will always be grateful for any ideas and suggestions.

www.goldfinchbooks.de

1st edition July 2007

ISBN 978-3-940258-03-8

Penzance
and West Cornwall

Julia Kaufhold
with illustrations by Nicola Clark

St Michael's Mount
Mousehole
Minack Theatre
Newlyn
Merry Maidens
St Ives
Land's End

and more

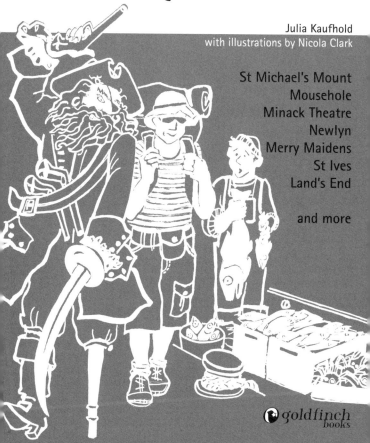

goldfinch
books

CONTENTS

ALL ROADS LEAD TO PENZANCE

As unromantic as it may sound – two of Penzance's main attractions are its station and its bus terminal. They make the town the **ideal touring base**, in which all modes of transport meet and then branch out again. All the nooks and crannies of the Penwith or Land's End peninsular can best be reached from Penzance, thus travellers usually pitch camp in this safe haven and then fan out into the mighty landscape of West Cornwall.

How fortunate that this popular base is also **one of the most interesting and varied places in the Southwest**!

Penzance's colourful history is most tangible in Chapel Street, with its strange mix of historic buildings and quaint smugglers' pubs, and the diverse representatives of the former **artists' colony** are to be found

in the numerous top-class galleries here or in the neighbouring fishing town of Newlyn.

The hustle and bustle of this little harbour town with its attractive shops – ranging from clothes boutiques, delis and alternative book-stores through to second-hand and antique shops – **belie its modest size.** There is equal variety when it comes to restaurants and going out. You can scoff a take-away Cornish pasty or dine on freshly caught fish in a gourmet temple, whilst traditional pubs, sophisticated cocktail bars and pulsating clubs court the favour of night revellers.

If all this hurly-burly is too much then just saunter along **Cornwall's only promenade**, take in the impressive backdrop of **St Michael's Mount**, enjoy the **Mediterranean feel** of the place and inhale the scent of flowers that bloom all year round thanks to the mild climate.

1 Tourist Information Centre (TIC)
2 Acorn Arts Centre
3 Supermarket
4 Bank
5 Cinema
6 Post Office
7 Library
8 Morrab Gardens
9 Penlee Memorial Park
10 Penlee House Gallery & Museum
11 Exchange Gallery
12 Newlyn Art Gallery
13 Police
14 Hospital

Getting there

BY CAR

Turn off the M5 onto the A30 towards Exeter at Exit 31 (Exeter South). Then simply continue on the A30 past Launceston, Bodmin and Redruth, signposted now to Penzance. Follow the signs to Penzance Centre passing the heliport on your right. This road brings you straight into the town.

The A30 from Exeter to Penzance has usually been the slowest part of the journey. Thanks to the recent dualling at the critical bottleneck, this section of the journey is no longer a problem.

BY TRAIN

Penzance is excellently served by rail connections. The southernmost and westernmost station in England is the end of the line for the many routes from London, Birmingham and Dundee. The *Night Riviera Sleeper* from Paddington goes straight from London to Penzance.
- **Information**: on Tel. 08457-484950 or at www.national rail.co.uk. Book your tickets as early as possible, as they are far cheaper then.

BY COACH

Usually takes longer than by train, but can be cheaper. Prices and travel times on Tel. 08705-808080 or at www.nationalexpress.co.uk.

Journey times to Penzance

Departure from	By train	By coach
London	5.5 hrs	9 hrs
Cardiff	5.5 hrs	9 hrs
Birmingham	6 hrs	8.5 hrs
Liverpool	7.5 hrs	12.5 hrs
Newcastle	9.5 hrs	15.5 hrs

(The above journey times are approximate.)

BY AIR

Newquay Airport is 41 miles from Penzance and is served by the following airlines:

Air Southwest

Flies from Gatwick (from £35), Manchester, Leeds Bradford (both from £38 single), Bristol, Cardiff, Cork (all three from £27) and Dublin (from £30) – all prices including taxes and charges, www.airsouthwest.com.

Ryanair

From Stansted (from about £25 each way including taxes and charges). www.ryanair.co.uk. Book early!

Bearing in mind the short distance, travel by public transport from Newquay to Penzance is not exactly an edifying experience.

Four ways of getting out of Newquay:

■ **Coach**: Best option. By taxi or the No. 910 bus *(Summercourt Travel)* to Newquay's Manor Road stop. Onward journey by coach, journey time 1½ hrs, no changes, but fairly infrequent, from about £5.20 (www.national express.com).

- **Bus**: A little sightseeing tour of the villages. From the Manor Road stop take the No. 89 or No. 90 bus to Truro (about 50 min.), then spend another 1½ hrs on the No. 18/18A/18B to Penzance (www.firstgroup.com).
- **Train**: Journey time about 2¼ hrs, one change, from about £7.
- **Hire car**: *Europcar* (01872-266300) or *Hertz* (01637-860869) are right by Newquay Airport. Journey to Penzance about 45 min.

Accommodation

In and around Penzance there is a huge variety of places to stay. The following websites are particularly helpful if you want an overview and wish to make a targeted search for vacant beds in accordance with the various price classes and accommodation types:

- **www.go-cornwall.co.uk**: The official website of *Penwith District Council*, to which the Tourist Information Centres (TICs) belong. Many registered accommodation providers, including information on availability.

- **www.visit-westcornwall.com**: Similar to the previous site, as *Penwith District Council* is also behind it. Even more specifically tailored to the west of Cornwall.

- **www.penzance-hotels.co.uk**: *Penzance & District Tourism Association*'s website. Participating hotels and guesthouses in Penzance and the surrounding villages are listed with room prices. You can even refine your search for suitable accommodation, e.g. only hotels at the eastern end of the promenade.

- **www.cornwalltouristboard.co.uk**: VisitCornwall – the *Cornwall Tourist Board*'s official website, with hundreds of accommodation providers. Constantly updated information on vacant beds.

- The **Tourist Information Centre** is extremely helpful when you're looking for somewhere to stay (see 'A-Z of Tips for Visitors').

All prices below include breakfast unless stipulated otherwise.

HOTELS
View meets ambience
Mount Haven Hotel

What? The proximity of St Michael's Mount is almost unreal, and there are views not only from the wonderful oasis-like terrace. Mount Haven is luxurious without bragging about it. Beautiful rooms – most of them with a sea view, and some with their own patio or balcony. Choice dishes in the restaurant, and relaxation thanks to a range of holistic therapies. Stylistically a mixture of Indian silk and flowers from the fields, or – to quote the owner Orange – "egocentric".

How much? From £45 pppn in standard double room (low season) and from £54 in the high season.

Where? In Marazion, Turnpike Road, Tel. 01736-710249, www.mounthaven.co.uk.

Historic location
Union Hotel

What? History was written here. It was in 1805 in the present breakfast room – the imposing Trafalgar Suite, with its high ceilings, stucco and candelabras – that Nelson's death and the victory at Trafalgar were first publicly announced. The 28 rooms combine tradition with fluffy white towels, and some of them have a view of St Michael's Mount. There's nowhere in Penzance any more central, and it's also calm and has its own car park, restaurant, bar and pub. Very good value.

How much? £31.25 pppn in double rooms. Single rooms £37.50 pppn.

Where? Chapel Street, Tel. 01736-362319, www.unionhotel.co.uk.

Assured style

Abbey Hotel

Absolutely charming hotel with wonderfully appointed, surprisingly large rooms. Bursting with attention to detail and good taste. The owners are the former top model Jean Shrimpton and her husband. Atmospheric garden, bookcases everywhere, and a view of the harbour and across to St Michael's Mount. The website has good photos of every single room. In January 2007 the Abbey Restaurant, which is open to non-residents, received a Michelin star.   **What?**

£50–£90 pppn in double room, depending on season and choice of room.   **How much?**

Abbey Street (a turning off Chapel Street), Tel. 01736-366906, www.theabbeyonline.co.uk.   **Where?**

BED & BREAKFAST/GUEST HOUSES

Penzance is full of B&Bs of varying sizes. The biggest range is probably to be found in the Alexandra Road area, mostly in Victorian houses with beautiful facades and high ceilings.

Tradition with a modern touch

Chiverton House B&B

Recently refurbished Victorian granite house with beautifully decorated, well equipped, clean rooms (all with en suite bath). Calm but central location. The friendly and extremely helpful owners Sally and Alan provide many tips, and do a first-class breakfast. Parking/WiFi.   **What?**

£25–£28 pppn in double room, £30–£40 in single room.   **How much?**

9 Mennaye Road, Tel. 01736-332733, www.chiverton housebedandbreakfast.co.uk.   **Where?**

Pampering for the fastidious
Camilla House

What? Modestly calls itself a Bed & Breakfast, but in every respect offers the extras you would expect of a high-class hotel, viz collection from the station, a huge breakfast selection (incl. smoked fish, big cheeseboard, wide range of fruit, home-baked bread) and fresh dressing gowns. Exquisitely furnished rooms with sea view. Despite all the luxury, the approach is personal – at breakfast-time the owner Simon presents his special weather forecast, and he and his wife Susan individually help all the guests plan their activities. Car park/WiFi.

How much? £35–£37.50 pppn in double room.

Where? 12 Regent Terrace, Tel. 01736-363771, www.camilla house.co.uk.

Cosy and relaxed
The Dunedin
Eight strikingly furnished rooms in a Victorian house. **What?**
Linda and John create a pleasant atmosphere of wellbe-
ing and spoil their guests with their opulent breakfasts.
Very clean. Free internet access throughout the house.
£25–£30 pppn in double room; singles £27.50–£35. **How much?**
Alexandra Road, Tel. 01736-362652, www.dunedinhotel. **Where?**
co.uk (informative video on the website).

(YOUTH) HOSTELS IN CORNWALL
200 hostels in England and Wales belong to the *Youth Hostel Association* (YHA), and ten of them are in Cornwall. They are of a surprisingly
high standard and are in particularly beautiful buildings. Guests of all
ages welcome. Whet your appetite on the website: www.yha.org.uk.

Nearby YHA hostels
- **Land's End**: Cute little hostel – actually nearer Cape Cornwall than
  Land's End (luckily!). Half of the rooms have a sea view. Five min-
  utes to the coast path and starting point for spectacular cliff walks.
  From £14 pppn (without breakfast). Tel. 01736-787337.
- **The Lizard**: Luxurious hostel at the southernmost extremity of the
  British mainland, and the starting point for one of England's most
  beautiful cliff walks: the walk to Kynance Cove, where you feel as
  if you're in the South Seas. From £15.50 pppn (without breakfast),
  Tel. 0870-7706120.

Private Hostels
No uniform standard – can be very good (e. g. *The Blue Dolphin Backpackers* in Penzance), but are sometimes less enthralling. Comprehensive but impartial information on backpacking at www.backpaxmag.
com and www.backpackers.co.uk.

HOSTELS
Haunted house
YHA Castle Horneck

What? Great atmosphere in Georgian villa in the middle of the woods. Clean rooms with two to ten beds, excellent cooking facilities (though meals also available), nice café, washing machine, camping permitted. Allegedly haunted!

How much? From £15.50 pppn (without breakfast).

Where? Castle Horneck, Alverton (just under half an hour's brisk walk from the station, or take No. 342/343/344/346 bus), Tel. 01736-362666, www.yha.org.uk.

Astoundingly clean and tidy
The Blue Dolphin Penzance Backpackers

What? Great hostel with clean rooms in central location (short cut to the centre through Penlee Park). Extremely friendly and helpful staff. No more waiting outside the 'wet room', as every dormitory and storey is equipped with showers. The kitchen has all mod cons, and tea and coffee are free. Free WiFi (best signal in the kitchen).

How much? From £14 pppn (without breakfast).

Where? Alexandra Road, 01736-363836, www.pzbackpack.com.

Almost like Woodstock
In conversation with **Algie Newell**, manager of the **Blue Dolphin Backpacker Hostel**

How do you manage to stop the hostel getting too chaotic?
You do have to be careful who you let in. And I sometimes say, we've only got spaces in women's or men's dormitories, depending on the situation – even when that's not strictly true. Otherwise it's easy to end up like one of the hostels in Newquay.

What have been the highlights during your time as hostel manager?
Last year 20 people from Brittany practised in the garden in costume, playing traditional instruments. And we once had a Jimi Hendrix tribute band rehearsing in the lounge.

What do you particularly like about Penzance?
Above all the people. They're friendly, have time for each other and are welcoming to everyone. Penzance is a fairly green town. And the surroundings: in five minutes you're out in the wilderness.

Algie's Penzance tips:
Restaurant: *The Baba* (Western Promenade). "Wonderful Indian restaurant, though not that cheap. My recommendation: If you have a meal for two at lunchtime you only pay for the more expensive dish."
Pub Food: *Pirate Inn* (Alverton Road). "Lovely garden."
Pub: *Bath Inn* (Cornwall Terrace). "Traditional."
Café: *Honeypot* (Parade Street). "Good coffee, good food."

CAMPING

There are no end of campsites in the Penzance area. The price per pitch (tent/car plus two people) varies greatly. Many of these sites have a sea view, and pretty much all of them are in beautiful sur-  roundings – most of them surprisingly clean. Dog owners should always ask whether they're allowed to bring their canine friends with them, as dogs are often not permitted. Penzance TIC has a list of camping sites.

Bone Valley Park: Campsite closest to Penzance – about 1½ miles north of the town, in a very pretty valley. Small family business. £4 in the low season for two people plus tent, £4.50 in the high season. Parking free. In Heamoor, Tel. 01736-360313, www.cornwalltouristboard. co.uk/bonevalley.

The Old Farm: Small, clean, friendly campsite with sea view, only a few minutes from the beach. Mainly families. From £10 to £13.50 (July to early September) for a car/tent plus two people. Lower Pentreath, Pentreath Lane, Praa Sands, Tel. 01736-763221, www.theoldfarmpraasands. co.uk.

River Valley Country Park: 5-star site idyllically situated on a river bank. £8.50 (low season) to £17.50 (high season) per car/tent plus two people. In Relubbus, about 4 miles from St Michael's Mount. Inland. Tel. 01736-763398, www.rivervalley.co.uk.

SELF-CATERING

To the hoteliers' chagrin, self-catering accommodation is gaining in popularity. For longer stays (especially for cooking fanatics) these holiday homes are thoroughly recommendable, as you don't have to eat out in a restaurant, so it's easier on your wallet. Rentals are nearly always by the week – usually Saturday to Saturday. For July/August it's a good idea to book the previous autumn. One week in the high season (August) costs from about £360 in the bottom price bracket (small one-bedroom cottage/flat).

The **TIC brochure 'Go West!'** includes various providers who often just offer one property in Penzance and surroundings. In Penzance itself accommodation mainly seems to be in B&Bs and hotels, whereas most of the holiday cottages are a bit outside – in Marazion, Mousehole or further west.

Classic Cottages: Over 470 cottages in Cornwall – many in the vicinity of Penzance. Tel. 01326-555555, www.classic.co.uk.

Cornish Traditional Cottages: Friendly company offering 400 cottages in Cornwall, including some in Penzance, Marazion, Mousehole, Newlyn, Lamorna and Porthcurno. Tel. 01208-821666, www.cornishtraditionalcottages.com

Cornwall Seaside Holiday Cottages: With its four holiday lets, this Marazion based company has a small but choice offering. Tel. 01736-710424, www.cornwall-holiday-cottages.com.

Food

It's surprising what culinary gems are to be found gathered here at the far end of the country. **Penzance is even home to one of Cornwall's two Michelin-starred restaurants**, the *Abbey Restaurant*, which in January 2007 received a Michelin star. Perhaps one reason for the high quality is the direct vicinity of Newlyn, Cornwall's most important fishing port and one of the richest harbours in Great Britain – rich because expensive fish and shellfish are landed in Newlyn. Thus **scallops, crab, lobster, turbot and sole** are on the menu in nearly every restaurant, and the chefs try to outperform each other in their preparation of these fine fruits de mer: Scallops, for example, are available fried in oyster sauce, served with roasted hazelnuts and apples, grilled with couscous und pine nuts, drizzled with marmalade, dished up in a langoustine sauce or with marinated ginger, tossed in white wine or enhanced with sweet-chilli sauce. Sounds exciting?

A further strength of Penzance's chefs lies in their preparation of select desserts, the very names of which suffice to mobilise undreamed-of quantities of saliva. Many of them are served or filled with the delicious Cornish clotted cream. Even though you'll put on weight just glancing at these **naughty-but-nice sweets**, just don't worry about it for once! So leave plenty of room in your stomach!

Eating out in Cornwall is usually expensive – there's just no denying it. **Skinflint** thus recommends:

- Lower prices at or before certain times, so look out for **early-bird menus** and teatime or lunchtime specials (often advertised outside, e.g. *The Bakehouse*/Chapel Street).
- Go out for **lunch instead of an evening meal** – the same dishes often much cheaper.
- **BYO**: This is getting rarer and rarer, but a few places in Penzance are still not licensed to dispense alcohol (e.g. the *Mackerel Sky Café*/New Street). In some restaurants, even though they're fully licensed, you can still bring your own bottle and pay the £1 to £2 corkage. Enquire at the restaurant beforehand!
- Cheap and cheerful: Most pubs offer very good **bar meals**, which above all come in generous portions.

RESTAURANTS
A feast for your eyes
The Bay

If you really want to spoil yourself, The Bay is the ideal place to go. Stylish dining in an unobtrusively elegant and simultaneously relaxed atmosphere amidst paintings by local artists. Fantastic view over the rooftops and down to the harbour. First-class food including good vegetarian dishes, a carefully coordinated wine list and astonishingly big portions.

What?

11.30am–2pm (Mon–Wed), daily 6–9.30pm (last orders). Lunchtime opening less frequent in the winter.

When?

From £22 for a two-course evening menu, three courses from £27.

How much?

Briton's Hill (past the station towards Marazion, fourth on the left), Tel. 01736-366890, www.bay-penzance.co.uk.

Where?

Tip	On the third Sunday of every month there is a three-course menu for £18.50, comprising only local produce. Reservations necessary.

Vibrant

Cocos

What?	Whether you want a quick coffee, a few drinks in the evening or a posh dinner, Cocos has proven to be a reliable port of call. The bar offers delicious tapas, dishes with a hint of the Mediterranean and a good wine list. The fishcakes, which elsewhere are often a sad affair, are here top-quality, comprising potatoes, onions and, please note, pieces of fish.
When?	Brunch/Lunch 10.30am–2.30pm, evening meals from 6.30pm. Coffee and cakes all day.
How much?	Mains £9.50–£14 (organic Cornish rib-eye steak), Tapas £2–£6.
Where?	12–13 Chapel Street, Tel. 01736-350222, www.cocos-penzance.co.uk.

In discussion with **Nigel Waller, proprietor of the Boatshed**

At the age of 16 the present-day businessman and **champion of a better Penzance** came to town. "My parents had a hotel in Chapel Street", explains Nigel, who initially made his living from diving. In 1981 he bought the wood and granite building on the harbour and converted it into the legendary nightclub *Bosun's Locker*: "The biggest change in my life. What I particularly like about it: **it's far more sociable than diving for crabs and sea urchins.**"

Why this particular building? "Its history fascinated me. The harbour is the oldest part of Penzance, and merchants from all over the world used to sail to it. The building dates from the 18th century and was a warehouse at the time. There didn't use to be a street between the harbour and the houses, so ships could get up close and the goods could be swung through the window."

Two tips from Nigel:
Favourite beach: Gwenver Beach. Totally unspoilt beach with lots of locals and surfers.
Favourite walk: Traditional Good Friday walk from Mousehole to Lamorna.

Two in one
Boatshed
Dining by the harbour: downstairs modern wine bar, upstairs rustic restaurant with old ship's beams and genuine church pews – and you can eat excellently in either of them. Nearly all the ingredients used are of Cornish origin, and the fish is from just round the corner.

What?

Don't miss the char-grilled Cornish sirloin with caramel-ised onions! Families very welcome.

When?	April–September daily 11am–5pm and 6.30–10pm, or later if it's busy. October–March mainly at the weekends (ring up!).
How much?	Evening mains from £6.50 (pizza) to £15 (whole grilled sea bass with coriander/cashew-nut pesto).
Where?	Wharf Road (after the Ross Bridge), Tel. 01736-368845, www.boatshed.info.

Palms and steel

Bakehouse

What?	Popular restaurant offering modern British cuisine, plenty of fresh fish and a mouth-watering menu. Service in this family restaurant is friendly, the portions are generous and the decor is hip, featuring a successful marriage of steel, bright colours and fresh flowers. Dress code: long trousers and pullovers to allow unrestricted enjoyment of cosy and warm dining in the leafy palm courtyard.
When?	Mon–Sat from 6.15pm.
How much?	Evening mains from £9 to £21.50 (whole grilled Dover sole).
Where?	Old Bakehouse Lane, Chapel Street, Tel. 01736-331331, www.bakehouse-penzance.co.uk.
Tip	£12 for a two-course menu if ordered before 7.30pm or Sat before 7pm.

Who said it's a "dive"?

Navy Inn

What?	A pub with classical music – how does that work? A glance at the menu and the plates will suffice to tell you that this is a sophisticated restaurant. A few years ago the London chef Keir Meikle took over this harbour dive, since when there has been a dramatic improve-

ment in both ambience and food. You really should try
the Newlyn crab with lemon and coriander. Reservation
highly recommended.

Food 10am–10pm, drinks until 11pm.   When?
£7.50–£16. Newlyn crab (starter) £6.50.   How much?
Lower Queen Street, Tel. 01736-333232.   Where?

CAFÉS

CORNISH CREAM TEA

An absolute must for anyone visiting Penzance is a Cornish cream
tea, comprising scones, clotted cream and jam. Argument is rife both
about the origin of the cream tea (Cornwall or Devon) and the pro-
nunciation of the word 'scone' (short or long vowel), but as far as the
origin is concerned we'll plump for Cornwall.

Make it yourself:
Recipe for scones (8)
250 g self-raising flour
1 pinch salt
2-3 table spoons sugar
50 g unsalted butter in pieces
125 ml milk

Preheat oven to 220°C.
Mix flour, salt and
sugar in a bowl. Add
the butter in small
flakes. Gradually
blend in the milk
and knead into a
smooth dough. Let

the dough rest in the fridge for 15 min., then roll out to about 2 cm thick on a floured surface and cut out approx. 6 cm-diameter rounds with a glass or cup. Place on a baking tray lined with greaseproof paper and coat with milk. Bake in the middle of the oven for about 10 min., until the scones are golden brown.

Tip: Place on a grid and cover with a clean tea towel so the moisture doesn't escape. Allow the scones to cool a little, but serve warm. Delicious!

Clotted cream is normally made from unhomogenised cow's milk, but as this is not always available here is a replacement **recipe:**
Mix two parts of whole milk with one part of double cream. Heat this mixture in a pan for a few hours on minimum heat, until a skin forms. Do not stir! Leave the pan in a cool place overnight, and the next day scoop off the lumpy cream from the surface. Discard the rest of the milk or use it for another purpose.

An institution
Archie Browns

What?	Where would Penzance be without its Archie? The vegetarian/vegan café has already converted many a meat-eater, because everything here tastes good. The dishes on offer change daily, e.g. mango and sweet potato curry, mushroom burgers with home-made chutney and always top-notch salads. NB: It can get very busy.
When?	Mon–Sat 9.30am–5pm, breakfast 9.30–11am. In the summer sometimes open in the evening.
How much?	Lunch £3–£6.
Where?	Bread Street/corner of Old Brewery Yard (on the first floor above the linked healthfood shop), Tel. 01736-362828, www.archiebrowns.co.uk.

A firm favourite

Honeypot

The cosiest café in Penzance, with wide window seats and cushions to sprawl around on, wooden floor, fresh flowers on the tables and wonderful hot chocolate. The cakes are incomparable and the food is of restaurant quality. In the 19th century there was a bar here, and after WWI a café with the same name. No breakfast, but snacks such as croissants. **What?**

Mon–Sat 10am–6pm, meals approx. 12–4.30pm, coffee and cakes all day. **When?**

Cakes £1–£3.50, mains £6.25–£8.25. **How much?**

5 Parade Street (opposite the Acorn Theatre), Tel. 01736-368686. **Where?**

Dhyano – barista trainer at the Honeypot

Probably the only freelance Italian cappuccino mixer in the country, he came to Penzance in summer 2002 and fell in love – with the town and with Cornwall.

What exactly is it that you like so much about Penzance? It offers the **rare combination of culture and nature**. Towns in Italy have a lot of culture but hardly any nature, and at the seaside there's nothing but tourists. Cornwall is like the Mediterranean, and in Penzance there are things happening all year round – not just in the tourist season. It also has the best galleries in Cornwall: **Together, Penlee House and Newlyn Gallery are better than Tate St Ives**.

What do you do when you're not making coffee? I produce catalogues for galleries and art magazines on DVD on the *Bopdoq* label (www.bopdoq.co.uk).

Guaranteed feeling of wellbeing
Mackerel Sky Café

What?   In this relaxed café service is paramount; as a guest you immediately feel good. It is on two tastefully decorated storeys, and late risers are particularly welcome, as Stevie and her crew serve their fabulous breakfast all day long. The coffee, the gourmet sandwiches and the fresh fish dishes aren't bad either.

When?   Mon–Wed 9am–3pm, Thur–Sat 9am–9pm, Sun 10am–2pm.

How much?   Lunch from £3.50. BYO drinks.

Where?   45 New Street (street linking Market Jew Street and the harbour), Tel. 01736 366866.

Best view
Renaissance

What?   Not everything in a shopping centre is necessarily bad. The big busy café/restaurant/bar is impressive because of its fantastic view of the harbour and St Michael's Mount. Good spot for a shopping break, checking e-mails (WiFi), Mediterranean food or a few cocktails. Not exactly recommended: the veggie breakfast, dripping with fat.

When?   The opening hours are not entirely fixed. Breakfast definitely until 12pm, lunch 11.30am–4pm, evening meals 5.30–9.30pm. Every Wednesday evening live jazz.

How much?   Coffee £1.40, lunch under £10, evening mains £8–£15.

Where?   In the Wharfside Shopping Centre, Tel. 01736-366277.

TAKEAWAYS

From the sea to your mouth
Captain's Fish Bar

The best fish 'n' chips in Penzance, probably because everything is made fresh and does not lie around for a long time, as so often happens. Also home-made pizza, and you can eat in the shop.

What?

Varying opening hours, depending on the season. Roughly: in the winter Tue–Sat 5–9pm, in the high season Mon–Sat 12–11pm and Sun 5–9pm.

When?

Medium fish 'n' chips £4.20, pizza from £3.75.

How much?

62 Daniel Place (almost on the promenade), Tel. 01736-330333.

Where?

Variety guaranteed
Penzance Pasty Company/Lavender's

Pasty fans don't consider Penzance itself the best place in Cornwall to buy pasties. Nonetheless, Lavender's in Penzance have the tastiest and the least fatty pasties, and above all the biggest range (over 20 kinds). The weirdest of all has to be the ‚breakfast pasty' with sausage, bacon, egg and baked beans. The vegetarian wholemeal pasty is unfortunately a bit dry.

What?

9.30am–4.30pm, in the high season until 6pm (85 Market Jew Street).

When?

Traditional steak pasty £1.90

How much?

Two branches in Market Jew Street: Nos 8 and 85. Also at the station and at Lavender's Deli, 6a Alverton Street.

Where?

THE CORNISH PASTY

> *'Page: Wife, bid these gentlemen welcome. Come, we have* **a hot ven-**
> **ison pasty** *to dinner: come gentlemen, I hope we shall drink down all*
> *unkindness.'*
> From: William Shakespeare *The Merry Wives of Windsor*, 1597.

In Cornwall you just can't get away from Cornish pasties. These filled,
crescent shaped pastry pockets are available all over the place here,
and can involve every conceivable combination.

The pasty derives its typical shape from its origin as the **daily meal of
Cornish tin miners**. As tin mining often involved handling of the poi-
sonous substance arsenic and miners were unable to wash their hands
before every meal, to avoid poisoning they used to hold their pasties by
the crusty pastry edge, eat the filling and throw the rest away. Hence
Cornish pasties' thick crimping, which remains a feature.

Basic recipe for Cornish pasties
(four pasties)

Dough:
450 g strong plain flour
½ a teaspoon salt
100 g cold butter
100 g lard
(or 200 g butter)
approx. 175 ml cold water

First mix the flour with the salt in a large bowl. Then bit by bit work the chilled butter and the lard in well with your fingers. Whilst constantly stirring, add as little water as is necessary to create a workable and non-sticky dough. Knead thoroughly with cold fingers, shape into a ball and place in the fridge for 45 minutes.

Filling:
300 g chuck steak or skirt
600 g potatoes
1–2 swedes
1 big onion
Salt, pepper, sugar

Cut the raw steak, the potatoes and the swedes into very small pieces, chop the onion finely and mix all the ingredients well. Add up to four table spoons of water or stock if necessary. Spice well with salt, pepper and a generous pinch of sugar.

Remove dough from fridge, divide into four portions and roll out into rounds on a floured surface. The rounds should have a diameter of 20–23 cm.

Lay some of the prepared meat/vegetable mixture on one half of each of the rounds. Gently moisten the edges with cold water, fold the rounds of dough over and press together firmly. Coat with beaten egg and make holes in each pasty using a fork.

Bake at 220 °C in a preheated oven for about 20 minutes. Then reduce the temperature to 150 °C and bake for a further 20 minutes. Before serving let the pasties rest for ten minutes in the switched-off oven.

SHOPPING FOR FOOD

Fish *Plentiful & top-quality*
W. Stevenson & Sons

What? Freshly caught fish aplenty from Newlyn from the biggest private fishing fleet in Great Britain and its 150-man crew. Not to be missed: the renowned Newlyn crab, and megrim – a fairly flat Cornish fish similar to sole.

When? Wharfside: Mon–Sat 9am–5pm, Newlyn: Mon–Fri 9am–5pm, Sat 9am–12pm.

Where? Wharf Road (downstairs in the shopping centre) and in Newlyn, The Strand (opposite the lifeboat house), www.wstevensonandsons.co.uk.

Delicacies *Tasting allowed*
The Deli

What? Huge selection of high-quality specialities – many of them from the region and/or organically grown. Not to be missed: the unbeatable olives and the numerous unknown types of cheese – tasting is expressly encouraged. Great snacks such as sandwiches with organic Cornish Brie, walnuts, apricot & date chutney, salads and a delicious vegetable soup with pesto. The coffee is also good, and there's a nice urban vista from the bar stool.

When? Mon–Sat 8.30am–5pm.

How much? 100 g olives £1.95, sandwiches £2–£4 depending on size, salads £3.50–£5.50, soup £4.

Where? 27 Market Place, Tel. 01736-350223, www.finefoods cornwall.co.uk.

Lavender's Deli: Mon–Sat 9am–5pm, 6a Alverton Street (see also under 'Takeaways').

Full of goodness
The Granary
Wholefoods, also many organic products, vegetables, loads of nuts and organic wines. Tasty snacks to put straight in your hand, e.g. pizzas, potato patties and various savouries.
Mon–Sat 9am–5pm.
15d Causewayhead.

Healthy food

What?

When?
Where?

- **D.L. Tregenza:** Mon–Sat 8.30am–5.30pm, 6 Greenmarket.

Fruit und vegetables

- **Penzance Country Market**: Every Thur 8.30–11.45am, St John's Hall.
- **Farmers' Market**: Every Sat, Wharfside Shopping Centre, in the courtyard.

Weekly markets

- **Co-op**: 114–117 Market Jew Street, also Wherrytown/ Promenade and 18 The Strand/Newlyn.
- **The Little Shop**: 9a Alverton Terrace.
- **Spar**: 46 Market Jew Street.
- **Lidl**: Wherrytown/Promenade.
- **Tesco**: At the eastern approach to the town, Eastern Green/Branwell Lane roundabout.

Supermarkets

Culture

Entertainment

Shakespeare by starlight
Minack Theatre

What?	Open-air theatre high above the sea, nestled in the steep granite cliffs. For nearly fifty years Rowena Cade and a single assistant cut the stage and seating into the cliffs on her land with their own hands. Shakespeare's 'The Tempest' was performed here in 1932, and the theatre now stages 18 plays a season. The thundering of the waves, the sunset and the starry sky become part and parcel of the performance – a unique experience.
When?	Evenings Mon–Fri and matinees Wed and Fri June–Sept. Open to visitors all year round.
How much?	Tickets £7–£8.50, under-16s £4.50. Day visitors £3.50, under-16s £1.40, free of charge for the under-12s.

The Minack Theatre

Porthcurno – follow the signs. By bus No. 1 or No. 345 from Penzance to Porthcurno (35–60 min.), and from there about ¼ mile walk up the steep hill – plan return bus journey in advance. Tel. 01736 810181, www.minack.com.

Where?

Minack survival kit
- Cushion (otherwise unbearable sitting on the cold, hard stones). Or: for £1 you can hire an excellent cushion/backrest at Minack.
- Rug (even in the summer it can get pretty chilly in the evening)
- Thick pullover, jacket, and perhaps scarf and gloves*
- Umbrella (capes available at the theatre)
- Sunscreen for matinees
- Hot drink in a thermos
- Bottle of wine, corkscrew and glasses
- Picnic

*the author admittedly feels the cold

Culture in the church
Acorn Arts Centre

This former Methodist church is **West Cornwall's main events centre**, and presents top events from all areas of culture, including theatre, cabaret, music, dance, film, readings, lectures and workshops. The impressive space, with its high church ceiling and its gallery, seats 250. Once a week in the summer, nearby Penlee Park is used as a stage, and there's often jazz in the open air.

What?

Events usually start between 7pm and 8.30pm. Box office Tue–Fri 11am–3pm.

When?

£3 to £17, depending on the event.

How much?

Parade Street (goes off Chapel Street), Tel. 01736-365520 (Mon–Fri 9.30am–5pm), www.acornartscentre.co.uk.

Where?

Living room atmosphere
Penzance Arts Club

What?   It's great that Penzance has its Arts Club. It boasts an alternative and elegant ambience, and ever since 1994 all the arts have been promoted here. If you listen to music performances by the open marble fireplace or go to one of the Club's parties you'll feel like a guest in a comfortable living room in the world of Bohemia. The Georgian villa dating from 1781 also accommodates a good organic restaurant and seven B&B rooms.

When?   Every other Thur Café Frug (poetry readings and music to listen to and take part in – highly recommended!), every other Fri Groove Lounge (see chapter 'Nightlife'), first Sat of the month jazz, every other Sat salsa, Sun gay night.

How much?   £2–£5 (for non-members), depending on the event. B&B £70–£90 for two people in a double room (depending on the season, and with/without own bath).

Where?   Chapel Street (lower end), Tel. 01736-363761, www.penzanceartsclub.co.uk.

FESTIVALS
Golowan Festival

What?   The whole of Penzance goes mad at its unique **midsummer festival**. This is eight to ten days long, attracts over 60,000 visitors, is celebrated to the full and adheres to a long tradition. Back in the late 19th century the Celts in Penzance and Newlyn celebrated the longest day of the year with extended festivities, and ever since 1990 this practice has been impressively revived. The main event is **Mazey Day**, with its grand parade – a sort of Celtic carnival procession. The surrounding villages and various countries and **regions of Celtic origin are involved in the lively spectacle**, with their traditional instruments, costumes and enormous papier-mâché sculptures. Also a **huge programme of festival events** in every possible corner of town, including top-rate musical performances, street theatre, film screenings, walks, market stalls and fireworks by the harbour.

Eight to ten days in the latter half of June.   When?

No overall festival ticket, as you pay per event, but much   How much?
of it is free and outdoors.

Information on Tel. 01736-334675, www.golowan.org.   Where?

Newlyn Fish Festival

A day devoted to fish and the fishing industry. Newlyn's   What?
important role in fishing and sea travel is duly celebrated with a big fish market, cooking demonstrations, live music and art & craft stalls. Newlyn's fishing boats and many sailing boats lie at anchor in the harbour, and visitors are welcome on board. The highlight is the big exhibition of locally caught fish, which is auctioned right at the end. Including shark!

Always on the last Monday of August (bank holiday),   When?
9am–5pm.

Entry £4, children free.   How much?

Information on Tel. 01736-364324, www.newlynfish   Where?
festival.org.uk.

Sea, Salts & Sail – Mousehole Maritime Festival

Traditions related to fishing are colourfully kept alive   What?
here. In Mousehole – once one of the main fishing ports in southwest England – traditional fishing boats can be admired in the water and on land during this weekend. Plus Cornish folk music and dances, historic walks, cooking demonstrations, craft work and much more. Anyone wishing to stay in the village of Mousehole should book accommodation well in advance.

When?	Every other year for three days (Fri–Sun) at the beginning/middle of July.
How much?	Free.
Where?	Info on Tel. 01736-731655, www.seasalts.co.uk.

St Ives September Festival

What?	Two-week 'state of alert' in St Ives. Live music can be heard in every pub, poets recite on the streets, artists open up their studios and music emanates from the church. The programme encompasses classical music, folk, jazz, blues, rock, world music, poetry, readings, theatre, comedy, cabaret, lectures, film screenings, open studios and art exhibitions. Early booking of accommodation advised!
When?	Annually in the second and third week of September (Saturday to Saturday inclusive).
How much?	No overall festival ticket, as you pay per event, but much of it is in the pubs and free.
Where?	Information at www.stivesseptemberfestival.co.uk and from Martin Val Baker on Tel. 01736-366077.

GHOST WALKS

What?	Scary walks on the theme of ghosts and other creatures of the night with Ian Addicoat, who seriously calls himself a 'ghost-hunter'. Pretty tourist-oriented event, but it's nevertheless good fun learning something about Penzance's gruesome history.
When?	April–June Thur at 8.30pm, July–September Thur and Sun, likewise 8.30pm.
How much?	Adults £4, children £2.
Where?	Start at the Tourist Information Centre. Information on Tel. 01736-331206, www.ghosthunting.org.uk.

Sights

Market House with statue of Sir Humphry Davy
Attractive, though somewhat unfavourably sited with regard to traffic. The 1838 Market House (housing Lloyds Bank) marks the centre of Penzance. In its day this granite building, with its Ionian-columned entrance and lead dome, housed the town hall and the market. The stony-faced Sir Humphry Davy (1778–1829), who looks down Market Jew Street with his stern gaze, was a chemist, and perhaps the most famous inhabitant of the town. He discovered laughing gas and invented the miners' safety lamp, which can be seen in the statue's hand.

> **Holy headland**
> The name 'Penzance' is from the Cornish *pen* meaning 'head' or 'end', and *sans* meaning 'holy'.

CHAPEL STREET
Tuscan colonnades, Egyptian lotus flowers, Cornish granite – Chapel Street is a strange but highly successful mix of styles.

Egyptian House
A sign of the evident British craze for things Egyptian, this house was built in about 1836, and was based on the *Egyptian Hall* in Piccadilly. Thus Penzance now has a rather curious building with trapezoidal windows, much ornamentation and columns decorated with lotus flowers. The bright colours were added in the 1970s.

1 Egyptian House
2 Statue of Sir Humphry Davy
3 Market House
4 St Mary's Church
5 Wesleyan Methodist Chapel
6 Turks Head/Admiral Benbow
7 St Anthony's Gardens
8 Morrab Gardens
9 Penlee Memorial Park
10 Penlee House Gallery & Museum
11 Exchange Gallery
12 Newlyn Art Gallery

St Mary's Church

This rather heavy example of neo-Gothic architecture is not exactly a feast for the eyes. This is made up for by the wonderful view over Mount's Bay – especially from the adjoining graveyard. There used to be a mediaeval chapel where this 1835 church now stands. The interior of St Mary's was completely restored in 1985 following a big fire.

Wesleyan Methodist Chapel

Somewhat more appealing is the 1864 Methodist church – set back a bit from the street and opposite the *Turks Head*. The facade is reminiscent of the south, and no wonder, as the columned entrance and the blue portals are in imitation of the Tuscan style.

A brief history

In the 11th century the first fishermen settled in Penzance, and three hundred years later (1322) the inhabitants gained the right to hold a market.

In **1595** Penzance suffered a cruel blow when the **Spaniards attacked the locality and largely destroyed it**. Seven years previously the Spanish Armada had suffered a bitter defeat in its battle with the English, and Penzance's geographical location made it an easy target for their revenge. The fortification of the harbour was a reaction to the attack.

Penzance bounced back, and in 1614 it was officially declared a town. The port's **flourishing exports of Cornish tin attracted pirates** from all over the place who got wind of the rich booty.

The **construction of the railway line in 1859** boosted fishing, as the catches could now be transported to London and Manchester and sold on the markets there. The new rail connection also represented the **beginning of tourism**.

Smuggling – *a digression*
The majority of Cornish people are said to have been involved in the smuggling trade. According to records dating from 1598 pots, alcohol and salt (needed for preserving fish) were the chief items smuggled. In Chapel Street's **Turks Head** and **Admiral Benbow** pubs you can still see the **entrance to a secret underground tunnel**, through which **alcohol was smuggled from the harbour straight to the bars**.

BY THE WATER
Jubilee Pool
Chic lido in the Art Deco style. This fine pool, the triangular shape of which is said to be modelled on a seagull alighting on the water, is constructed on the rocks right next to the sea. It was built in 1935, and thus rode the

wave of the 30s, when the British erected a total of 169 outdoor pools. Most of them no longer exist, and of those that remain Penzance has one of the best. **The pool is filled with salt water, and thanks to its unique coastal location it is subject to sea tides.** Between the harbour and the promenade (Information on opening hours and prices in the chapter 'Activities').

Battery Rocks
There's a little path round the outside of the Jubilee Pool and facing the open sea – in the early 19th century there was an arsenal here. This is where hardy swimmers now plunge in every day of the year.

St Anthony's Gardens
Straight opposite the Jubilee Pool, on the site of the former 6th-century *Chapel of St Anthony*, is a further example of flourishing horticulture right in the town centre. Named after the patron saint of fishermen and seafarers, the park includes a large fountain hewn from a single piece of granite.

The Promenade
Cornwall's only promenade follows the water all the way to Newlyn. Though it now seems unbelievable, there were once dunes here where fishermen brought in their catches and mended their nets. The Promenade was built in 1840, and twenty years later the fishermen were prohibited from using the beach below it – the idea being to allow the newly arrived tourists to undress without disturbance.

Further sightseeing
- Morrab Gardens and Penlee Memorial Park in the chapter 'Gardens'
- Penlee House Gallery & Museum in the chapter 'Art'

Art Mecca

Penzance has become a Mecca for professional artists, collectors and art enthusiasts. It doesn't matter whether you prefer the Old Masters or current trends – **Penzance has everything, and the very best of everything**. Far from the world of kitsch, in Penzance's many galleries you can now find what goes to make up Cornish contemporary art: expressiveness, versatility and freshness. The re-opened *Newlyn Art Gallery* and the new *Exchange* art venue (both 2007) form the highlights with regard to contemporary art. *Penlee House Gallery & Museum*, which specialises in *Newlyn School* artists, is the excellent historic equivalent.

PAINTING IN NEWLYN

When art in Penzance is mentioned, this always includes Newlyn. In the late 19th and early 20th century an artists' colony of a high calibre formed in this little fishing village, with its ideal location on the southwestern edge of Penzance. The 'Newlyn Society of Artists', the 'Newlyn School' and the 'Newlyn School of Painting' are fundamental in this context:

Newlyn Society of Artists

The Newlyn Society of Artists is an internationally renowned **society of over 100 professional artists** who live either in the Westcountry or have a close link with the region. The majority of its members are painters, though some are printmakers, sculptors, photographers and video and installation artists. The society's home gallery is the 'Newlyn Art Gallery', but members' exhibitions can also be seen at other locations in Penzance, in Cornwall, in London, and even outside the UK.

The Newlyn Society of Artists was founded back in 1896 by a group of painters who organised joint exhibitions in the 'Newlyn Art Gallery', which had been built the year before. These locally resident artists and founder members later became known as the 'Newlyn School'.

Cornwall's answer to impressionism
Newlyn School
'Newlyn School' describes the style associated with the artists' colony in Newlyn from 1882 until the 1930s. Inspired by trips to Brittany and in search of similar landscapes back in England, artists deemed Newlyn to be the ideal place.

"Newlyn is a sort of English Concarneau and the haunt of a great many painters." (Stanhope Forbes shortly after his arrival in Newlyn in a letter to his mother, 1884)

Newlyn meant **breathtaking light**, a wide variety of subject matter and, last but not least, cheap accommodation. The down-to-earth nature of the inhabitants fascinated the artists, as did the fact that they made a living from the sea. **Painting was done outside**, in natural light. This practice – cultivated at the time in France – became the Newlyn artists' guiding principle.

Newlyn School of Painting
Towards the end of the 19th century the number of artists in Newlyn decreased, prompting the first-generation Newlyn artists Stanhope and Elizabeth Forbes to found a school of art in 1899. One of their goals was to **keep**

the artists' colony alive, and the other was to pass on their own experiences and what they had learnt. The School of Painting did indeed attract many new artists to the little coastal village, including Ernest and Dod Procter, Sir Alfred Munnings, Harold and Laura Knight and Lamorna Birch, who later went down in art history as the **second generation of Newlyn and Lamorna artists.** The painters of the late Newlyn School often used landscapes as independent subject matter, and they more often painted in the studio using models from London instead of locals. The Forbes' School, as it was also known, comprised three studios in the centre of the village, one of which – scandalously – was reserved for life drawing. The Newlyn School of Painting, which also formed the social focus of the artists' colony, existed until 1938.

Newlyn School – its artistic ideals:
- **Painting 'en plain air'**, i.e. not in the studio but outside
- Depicting 'real life' precisely and not dressing it up – creating a kind of record for one's descendants
- Subject matter: people in their natural surroundings and their tough everyday existence, **tragedies experienced by fishermen and seafarers**, children at play, village life
- Style: muted colours, subtle shades, structured surfaces and blurred contours through use of square-ended brushes

NEWLYN ARTISTS (a selection)

Walter Langley (1852–1922): The first artist to settle in Newlyn, in 1882. The trained lithographer became well known for his extraordinary watercolour technique, which he used to portray the tough everyday life of fishermen and their families.

Stanhope Alexander Forbes (1857–1947): One of the leading lights of the artists' colony in Newlyn and founder of the *Newlyn School of Painting* together with his wife Elizabeth Forbes. A visit to Brittany in the early 1880s brought the Dublin-born artist into contact with the new 'plein air' painting, which he henceforth devoted himself to heart and soul.

Elizabeth A. Forbes, née Armstrong (1859–1912): Following travels throughout Europe (using a studio on wheels in Brittany), in 1889 the Canadian artist settled in Newlyn, where, inspired by French realism she above all painted children. The 'Queen of Newlyn', as her obituary described her, was more avant-garde and stylistically more versatile than her husband, and during her lifetime she sold more work than most of her male contemporaries.

Samuel John 'Lamorna' Birch (1869–1955): A representative of the second generation of Newlyn artists, this autodidact moved to the Lamorna valley in 1902. The passionate fisherman painted in the open air in oils and watercolours, and adopted the nickname ‚Lamorna' to differentiate himself from his fellow painter Lionel Birch. He is described as the father of the late *Newlyn School*.

Dame Laura Knight (1877–1972): The first female artist to be knighted (!) and elected as a member of the *Royal Academy*. From 1907 to 1919 she and her artist husband Harold Knight mainly lived and worked in Lamorna. She was a main figure of the late Newlyn artists' colony, and her subject matter is frequently landscapes with people (also life models).

GALLERIES
Flagship for Penzance
Penlee House Gallery & Museum

The town's cultural highlight. In a big exhibition space, visitors can marvel at **first-class work by representatives of the Newlyn School** and the Lamorna Group (1880–1930). There is no permanent exhibition of Penlee's own collection, but to complement the extremely interesting changing exhibitions, works by Norman Garstin, Elizabeth Forbes and Walter Langley are always on show. Penlee also has an archaeological department and a collection illustrating the social life of Penzance from 1600 to the present day. The **bright white Penlee building, situated in the middle of a park landscape**, is in itself worth a visit. Penzance's affluent Branwell family had the Victorian Villa built in 1865 as a private dwelling. In 1997 it was totally renovated. Shop and charming café *(The Orangery)*.

What?

PENLEE HOUSE
Gallery & Museum
PENZANCE

When?	Good Friday–September: Mon–Sat 10am–5pm, entry until 4.30pm. October–Maundy Thursday: Mon–Sat 10.30am–4.30pm, entry until 4pm. Closed on Sundays.
How much?	£3 for adults, reductions £2, children free. Entry free on Saturdays.
Where?	Morrab Road, Tel. 01736-363625, www.penleehouse.org.uk.

Where everything began

Newlyn Art Gallery

What?	Cornwall's leading publicly funded art gallery exhibits top regional, national and international contemporary art in all media. Following 18 months of extensive modernisation and expansion the gallery, which was built in 1895, reopened in July 2007. The stylish new two storey glass pavilion has sea views, and houses an art bookshop, an education room and a café.
When?	Summer: Mon–Sat 10am–5pm, Sun 11am–4pm. Winter: Mon/Tue closed.
How much?	Entry free.
Where?	Newlyn, New Road. On the road from Penzance, on the left as you enter Newlyn. Tel. 01736-363715, www.newlynartgallery.co.uk.

Superlative art venue

The Exchange

What?	Behind the wave-shaped glass frontage lies what is probably Penzance's biggest art project of recent years. In summer 2007 Newlyn Art Gallery opened a de luxe art venue in the heart of Penzance, complementing its home gallery in Newlyn. Works by leading contemporary regional, national and international artists are displayed in an exhibition area twice the size of that in Newlyn. **The biggest contemporary gallery within a radius of 180 miles**, it also boasts a shop and a very attractive

café, plus an education wing with workshop, offering a wide range of courses.

Summer: Mon–Sat 10am–5pm, Sun 11am–4pm. Winter: Mon/Tue closed.

When?

Entry free.

How much?

Princes Street, Tel. 01736-363715, www.theexchange gallery.co.uk.

Where?

Finger on the pulse

Cornwall Contemporary

This light gallery with its minimalist fittings, which opened on 1st September 2006, has rapidly blossomed into a showplace for Cornwall's really big contemporary artists. Ever since graduating from *Falmouth College of Art* in 1996 the owner Sarah Brittain has regularly been involved in art – as an illustrator of children's books, an organiser of various art projects and the author of art books and catalogues. Her gallery mailing list already contains 1,300 addresses, and every three to four weeks Brittain dishes up a new exhibition, **causing art collectors to lick their lips in anticipation**. In so doing, she always keeps her eyes open for promising newcomers to the scene.

What?

Mon–Sat 10am–5pm.

When?

1 Parade Street, on the corner of Chapel Street, Tel. 01736-874749, www.cornwallcontemporary.com.

Where?

Cornish by nature

Rainyday Gallery

Martin Val Baker's gallery houses a huge range of works by excellent Cornish artists. The St Ives-born gallery owner and former printer has put on over 170 exhibitions since 1992. His selection does not adhere to any uniform style – **he exhibits whatever takes his fancy, and the collectors evidently like that**. A fair-sized se-

What?

lection of works by well-known local artists is always on show, including pictures by Matthew Lanyon, a hundred or so of whose works Baker has already sold. Also art postcards, books and ceramics.

When? Mon–Sat 10am–5pm.

Where? 22 Market Jew Street, Tel. 01736-366077, www.rainy daygallery.co.uk.

**Rainyday Gallery owner
Martin Val Baker** – an insider's view

Cornish art today

"This is an exciting time for art in Cornwall," says Baker – "it's a clash between the generations". The most obvious example of the succession of generations must be the Frost family: Sir Terry Frost (1915–2003), his son Anthony and his grandson Luke – all of them top painters. During his childhood in St Ives Baker played cricket with Frost's sons: „The many years of contact are a great help."

Abstract art

"When people stand somewhat uncertainly in front of an abstract painting and ask: 'What's it supposed to mean?', I say to them: '**It's like a language you've not yet learnt**. To understand it you have to keep on consciously looking at abstract pictures.'"

Pricing

The prices in Martin Val Baker's gallery range from £100 to £5,800, 40% of which goes into his pocket. "In London gallery owners often take 60% of the sale price," he says.

The prices are determined by the artists themselves, but sometimes Baker has to give them 'cautious tips': "For example, when artists try to improve their reputation by raising the prices of their works." Or the opposite may apply: "Sometimes I have to say to artists that they can't sell anything here for under £100."

Music promotion
The son of the author Denys Val Baker has not devoted himself solely to visual arts – he is equally committed to music, and books lavish bands for the annual Golowan Festival and St Ives September Festival (see chapter 'Entertainment').

Expressive, varied and occasionally provocative
Goldfish Contemporary Fine Art
One of the biggest private galleries in Penwith. The **What?** owner Joseph Clarke presents Cornish contemporary art – abstract and representational painting, sculptures and installations – on three floors. The authenticity and personal expression of the artists is always in the foreground – pulsating and inspiring. His biggest coup: Simultaneously with the Tate St Ives exhibition 'Art Now Cornwall' (spring 2007) Clarke put on a show of the same name, but ending in a question mark, questioning and challenging the Tate's selection criteria for their exhibition.

Mon–Sat 10am–5pm. **When?**
56 Chapel Street, Tel. 01736-360573, www.goldfish **Where?** fineart.co.uk. (You can read about the debate on 'Art Now Cornwall' at www.artcornwall.org.uk (forum).)

The pearl of Newlyn
Badcocks Gallery
In the immediate vicinity of Newlyn's busy harbour area **What?** is one of Cornwall's leading galleries for contemporary

art. Between March and November there is a new exhibition every three weeks. Sculptures, a good selection of jewellery, craft work and ceramics are also displayed.

When? | Mon–Fri 10.30am–5.30pm and Sat 11am–5.30pm.
Where? | Newlyn, The Strand. Tel. 01736-366159, www.badcocks gallery.co.uk.

Galleries Guide

What? | Ever since 1994 Martin Val Baker has been publishing a comprehensive booklet – now containing 80 pages – that provides an overview of 150 galleries in Cornwall and Devon. It also covers crafts, museums, bookshops etc., all of them indicated on town maps.
How much? | £1.
Where? | The booklet is available at the *Rainyday Gallery* (address see above) and most other galleries.

SCHOOL OF ART
Penzance School of Art

What? | Not everyone knows this: Long before the first artists had settled in Newlyn Penzance formed a centre for art, thus becoming the first town west of Bristol to have an art school. Opened back in 1853, the school was and is intended for everyone, though various famous personages taught and learnt here, e.g. the father of English ceramics Bernard Leach and the abstract painter Peter Lanyon. The school is now part of *Penwith College*, and offers interesting art and craftwork courses of every hue.
Where? | Morrab Road, next to the library. Tel. 01736-335000.

ARTISTS' REQUISITES
The Art Shop
Anyone suddenly taken by the muse as a result of the   What?
wealth of fabulous subject matter will find everything
a creative artist might possibly need in Peter and Mary
Noall's well-stocked shop.
Mon–Sat 9am–5.30pm.   When?
57 Chapel Street, Tel. 01736-366437.   Where?

ART-TRIP TIPS
Tate St Ives
One of the four Tate galleries, the others being Tate   What?
Modern and Tate Britain in London and Tate Liverpool.
Tate St Ives was **opened in 1993 by Prince Charles**, and
shows modern art in a Cornish context. The gallery's
own collection comprises **works by all the relevant artists who have worked in St Ives**. Changing exhibitions
of national and international contemporary art and ceramics. What makes Tate St Ives so attractive is proba-

bly the almost magical relationship between its dynamic architecture, its mighty surroundings and its exhibits, which reflect this interplay. The gallery has an enormous influence on tourism (and unfortunately on traffic in St Ives).

When? March–October: Mon–Sun 10am–5.20pm, entry until 5pm. November–February: Tue–Sun 10am–4.20pm, entry until 4pm.

How much? £5.75 for adults, reductions £3.25, free entry for the under-18s and over-60s. (Tate and Hepworth Museum with a combined ticket cheaper than with single tickets.)

Where? In St Ives, right on Porthmeor Beach, www.tate.org.uk/stives.

Barbara Hepworth Museum & Sculpture Garden

What? Barbara Hepworth's studio and sculpture garden, where she lived and worked from 1949 onwards until her death in 1975 as a result of a fire in her studio. You can now view her sculptures, paintings, drawings, private photos and letters here. **Her workshops have been left exactly as they were**, and the tools, overalls and half-worked stones lying around give the impression that Hepworth has just left the room for a moment. Hepworth's sculpture garden, in which **she personally positioned most of her bronze sculptures amidst tropical plants**, is an oasis of calm (provided there aren't too many visitors).

When? Same opening hours as Tate St Ives.

How much? £4.75 for adults, reductions £2.75, free entry for the under-18s and over-60s.

Where? In St Ives, Barnoon Hill, www.tate.org.uk/stives/hepworth.

Art website

- **www.artcornwall.org.uk:** Anyone wishing to know what artists and gallery owners in Cornwall are currently up to, will find everything they need to know here. It was in 2006 that Rupert White, an artist from Penzance, started this ambitious online magazine about art in Cornwall. The site features reflections on **everything connected with art in the region – and that's a lot!** The site uses typical magazine headings such as exhibition reviews, interviews and artist profiles, and boasts a much frequented forum at which artists, gallery owners and other interested parties can swap ideas and opinions.

Literature

LIBRARIES

Penzance Library

Publications on all topics, especially art and things Cornish, plus specialist books, current newspapers and numerous Internet stations.

What?

Mon–Fri 9.30am–6pm, Sat 9.30am–4pm. On Wed/Thur 3.30–5pm the computers are reserved for schoolchildren (not in the summer holidays).

When?

Internet for members £2/hr (first half hour free), for non-members £3, charged in 15-minute units. Deposit on loans for visitors usually £10.

How much?

62 Morrab Road, Tel. 01736-363954.

Where?

Morrab Library

Everything imaginable, ranging from novels to publications on Cornish/Celtic topics, newspapers and a (photo) archive. Frequent lectures and talks in the winter.

What?

Tue–Fri 10am–4pm, Sat 10am–1pm, Sun/Mon closed.

When?

Day membership for visitors £5, otherwise £25 a year.

How much?

In the Morrab Gardens, Tel. 01736-364474, www.morrablibrary.co.uk.

Where?

BOOKSHOPS
Penzance Bookshop
What?   One day a gentleman entered the shop and introduced himself as John Burley, author of the Cornish crime-thriller series *Wycliffe*, and asked whether he could set his next novel in Penzance Bookshop. 'Wycliffe and the Cycle of Death' (1990) really is set here in the shop, where the proprietor is mysteriously killed. The real bookseller Tim Wallace is fortunately alive and kicking and sells above all, but not exclusively, books on art and history with a local/regional connection, and specialises in maps.

When?   Mon–Sat 9.30am–5pm.
Where?   5 Chapel Street, Tel. 01736-365444.

Books Plus
What?   Thematically wide-ranging, busy independent bookshop with a special focus on books from and about Cornwall.

When?   Mon–Sat 9am–5.30pm.
Where?   23 Market Jew Street, Tel. 01736-365607.

Penzance Rare Books
What?   Old books, wooden shelves, a subtle mustiness – you've just got to be able to experience antiquarian bookshops with your senses. As well as out-of-print publications, this well stocked shop also sells second-hand books on every conceivable topic – above all art. If you can't find what you're looking for, Patricia and her team will give you useful tips to help you with your own (Internet) research.

When?   Mon–Sat 10.15am–5pm.
Where?   43 Causewayhead, Tel. 01736-362140.

Kelvin and the kicking artists
Kelvin Hearn, proprietor of Newlyn Books

It is rare for a bookseller to be an enthusiastic football player, and the fact that five of Kelvin's kicking colleagues are working artists is a phenomenon that is probably only possible in a town like Penzance.

This sporting book enthusiast has lived here for 22 years, and knows the **'hotbed of culture' – as he calls Penzance** – like the palm of his hand. Here are his top tips:

Gallery: *Penlee House* and *Goldfish Gallery*.

Restaurant: *Bakehouse* and *Navy Inn* – a pub with high-quality food.

Pub: *Turks Head*. Nice old-fashioned atmosphere and no TV. Good beer, open fire and pretty garden.

Coffee: At *Cocos*.

Place: *Mounts Bay Rugby Club* in Alexandra Road. Home game every other week.

Walk: Zennor to St Ives and back through the fields. I go off walking every weekend, so I've got a lot of favourite routes.

Book: Arthur Ransome's series of children's books 'Swallows and Amazons'. I've him to thank for my love of reading. I lap up his books time and again.

Newlyn Books

Good antiquarian/second-hand bookshop on two storeys in Penzance's first post office, dating from 1830, when stamps were not yet in use. Wide range of topics, with an emphasis on Cornish subject matter, art, design and illustrated books. Also new publications on Cornish topics. Lovely postcards by local artists.

What?

| When? | Mon–Sat 10am–5pm. |
| Where? | 9 Chapel Street, Tel. 01736-332266. |

NOVELS SET IN PENZANCE AND ENVIRONS

- **W.J. Burley**: *Wycliffe*: Charles Wycliffe is a sort of Cornish Inspector Morse. These **crime thrillers** are exciting, and are always set in well known Cornish locations – the 1990 volume *Wycliffe and the Cycle of Death* actually being set in *Penzance Bookshop* in Chapel Street. In the 90s the books were made into a 36-episode TV series. Burley died in 2002 near Newquay. (Good website on the author and his books: www.wjburley.com.)

- **Jonathan Smith**: *Summer in February* (1995): A quasi-biography of the Lamorna-based artist Sir Alfred Munnings. The dramatic action is **set in pre-WWI Newlyn and Lamorna**, when Munnings was part of the **local artists' colony**. The storytelling is so vivid as to make readers feel they are personally experiencing the landscape, air and light.

- **Daphne du Maurier novels**: Though not set in the immediate vicinity of Penzance, they do deserve to be mentioned, as du Maurier understands like no other author how to interweave Cornwall's mystic landscape with her thrilling stories. *Jamaica Inn* (1936), *Rebecca* (1940) and *My Cousin Rachel* (1951) are particularly recommended.

- **Rosamunde Pilcher novels**: Penzance is the most frequently mentioned town in the novels. *The Day of the Storm* and *The Empty House*, for example, are set here, and reliably enough they have happy endings, as we have come to expect from the author, who was born in Lelant (West Cornwall) in 1924.

- **Patrick Gale novels**: Gale, who lives on a farm near Sennen, writes novels featuring **dramatic interaction between the raw Cornish landscape and his protagonist's psyche**. In his fifteenth novel *Notes from an Exhibition* (2007), the action of which is set around Penzance, the main figure is the bipolar artist Rachel. Sounds hard, but makes for captivating holiday reading.

Patrick Gale, West Cornwall-based author: "Because my novels are very much about psychology and relationships, the landscape affects the writing all the time. Your moods project onto the landscape and the landscape projects back onto you, so **good landscape writing is really about states of mind.**"

© Judy Duckworth, *Cornwall Today*, April 2007.

NON-FICTION ON PENZANCE-RELATED TOPICS

- **Clive Carter**: *The Port of Penzance* (1998): History entertainingly told. The historian Carter brings back to life the **legends of the harbour town** connected with smugglers, pirates and military conflicts. Includes 175 photographs, drawings and maps.

- **Philip Payton**: *Cornwall – A History* (2004): Not a boring historical summary but an exciting, apt and really amusing book describing the Cornish identity, the secret of the Celts, the ancient sites and the Cornish language, and considering the state of Cornwall today. Payton is Director of the Institute for Cornish Studies at Exeter University. **Definitely THE book on the history of Cornwall.**

- **Tom Cross**: *Shining Sands – Artists in Newlyn and St Ives 1880–1930* (2007): Well written book on the founding and development of the artists' colonies in these two Cornish fishing villages, from the arrival of the first artists through to the outbreak of WWII.

- **Sue Lewington books**: Genuine artworks in book form. The artist Lewington loves Cornwall and has dedicated a picture to almost every corner of the county. The resultant beautiful little books, e.g. *Looking Westward. St Ives to Land's End* (2001) and *Mousehole* (2003), are collectors' items.

LITERATURE SIGHTSEEING
Branwell House

What? The house where Maria Branwell, **mother of the authors Charlotte, Emily and Anne Brontë**, spent her childhood. This red-brick building – erected c. 1780 – is atypical of the region. In its day the so-called Rotterdam style indicated a high social status.

Where? 25 Chapel Street.

WRITING HOLIDAYS
Pushing creative buttons

What? In the inspiring ambience of the Arts Clubs and its stimulating environs, it is not hard to find reasons for creative writing. Under the professional tutelage of poet and playwright Phil Bowen, groups of two to ten people are encouraged to write. Suitable for beginners and advanced writers alike. For artists, the Arts Club offers similar painting holidays (numerous techniques and levels).

When? On enquiry.

How much? From £100 for a one-day course, including B & B. Longer workshops also offered.

Where? Penzance Arts Club, Chapel Street, Tel. 01736-363761. Information also from the course leader Phil Bowen, Tel. 01736-360531.

Music

LIVE MUSIC

If you wanted you'd have no problem hearing live music in Penzance every evening. And that's not only because in the *Studio Bar* alone there are performances seven evenings a week – the various pubs also offer **live music to go with the beer**.

You're welcome to join in
Pirate Inn

In a former farmhouse, every Tuesday there's a jam session for folk musicians, who like it if guests simply join in. Every Thursday there's live music, mainly rock, pop and blues. The friendly pub has a big, atmospheric garden and very good food.   **What?**

10.30am–11.30pm, music approx. 9–11pm. Tue eve: Folk jam session; Thur evening: Live music.   **When?**

Beer £2.40–£2.60 a pint. Mains (evenings) £7–£14 (fillet steak).   **How much?**

Alverton Road, Tel. 01736-366094, www.pirateinn.co.uk.   **Where?**

The Guinness flows freely
Flanagan's Bar

Irish pub with live gigs at least twice a month – more often in the summer. Mainly blues and jazz, but also rock and pop. Individual vocal experimentation at the karaoke every Thursday.   **What?**

The music usually starts at 8.30pm (Fri/Sat and sometimes Sun), and you're booted out at 1am.   **When?**

Beer £2.40 to £2.78 a pint.   **How much?**

3 East Terrace, at the bottom of Market Jew Street, opposite the station, Tel. 01736-363181.   **Where?**

A guest of ...
... Alex Rutherford in the **Studio Bar**

A memorable date: On 1st November 2006 Alex Rutherford opened the Studio Bar, which in a very short time has made its name as **Penzance's top club for live music**.

"The bar was actually meant for musicians I was working with in the daytime in the recording studio," explains Alex. This is a familiar set-up for the expert sound engineer from London. **He has recorded top musicians including no less than George Harrison, Ringo Starr, Eric Clapton and Tina Turner** in the capital, where each studio has its own bar.

"Here in Penzance I had long used a mobile recording studio in a truck, and in the evenings the musicians always used to come back home with me – until my wife at some stage suggested I start my own studio."

The bar that goes with it came into being more quickly than the actual recording space, and it now offers a platform for musicians and other performers.

"Every day I get two or three emails from all over Europe from people who want to perform here. I just don't have the time to listen to everything."

No wonder! Particularly at weekends it's full to bursting in the fair-sized bar, and Alex is responsible for the ingenious sound system – he is, after all, an expert.

Seven nights a week
The Studio Bar

What?   THE venue for live music in Penzance. Every single evening there are musicians performing in this comfortable and somewhat rough bar atmosphere. Mon: Acoustic Night; Tue: Electric Jam Night; Wed: Acoustic; Thur: Blues; Fri: Jazz; Sat: Varying artists; Sun: Acoustic/Folk. Internet café plus WiFi Hotspot.

Daily 9am–1.30am. **When?**

Entry always free. Internet £1/hr. **How much?**

40–41 Bread Street, opposite Belgravia St. NB: Easy to miss! Tel. 01736 369724 or 07720-498480 (Alex), www.studiobar.com (Live relay of gigs on the net). **Where?**

Go and grab the mike
Dock Inn
Every Sunday in the early evening the house band let you tear their guitars from their hands. At the 'Open Mic' anybody who feels a calling for singing rock numbers can take the mike. Never fear – the harbour pub only appears frightening at first, but once you're in the thick of it you'll soon feel at home. **What?**

Mon–Wed 12–11pm, Thur–Sun 12pm–12am. Sun from 5.30pm 'Open Mic'. **When?**

Beer £2.45–£2.70 a pint. **How much?**

17 Quay Street, right by the harbour, Tel. 01736-362833. **Where?**

There's always **live jazz** on the first Saturday of the month in the Arts Club (see chapter 'Entertainment') and every Wednesday evening at *Renaissance* (see under 'Cafés').

There's also a lot of music at the Acorn Arts Centre (see 'Entertainment'), where mainly **singer/songwriters** and **tribute bands** are presented, and occasionally something more exotic.

CLASSICAL MUSIC

Penzance is not exactly a mecca for classical music, but the little there is, is of the highest standard.

International Musicians Seminar (IMS)

What? Every spring (usually around Easter) and every September the IMS puts on classical concerts in a few churches around Penzance. The IMS operates from nearby Prussia Cove, a former smugglers' haunt. It was founded in 1972, and twice a year **top musicians from various countries** come to courses and play together. Chamber music for strings and piano is the standard fare.

When? Six concerts in April, and nine on the last three weekends of September.

Where? Including St Buryan, St Michael's Mount, St Erth, St Ives and Paul (a village near Mousehole). Infos and tickets on Tel. 0207-7209020 (Rosie), www.i-m-s.org.uk.

St Mary's Church

There are a fair number of classical concerts here. The TIC will have the current dates (Tel. 01736-362207). Also watch out for notices in front of the church. Chapel Street. All concerts at St Mary's are listed at www.cofepenzance.org.uk ('What's on').

INSTRUMENTS AND MUSIC

For guitar aficionados

Mount's Bay Music

What? It's blatantly obvious that this packed shop focuses on guitars. It's the only shop in Penzance supplying sheet music, and it has a good selection of folk instruments such as banjos and mandolins, plus wind and string instruments.

When? Mon–Sat 10am–5pm.

Where? 39 Causewayhead (at the top on the right), Tel. 01736-333500.

Film

CINEMA
Savoy Penzance

Penzance boasts a cinema with three screens. Opened in 1912, it is the oldest continuous running cinema in the UK. It usually shows current blockbusters, and twice a week (Mon/Sun) the *Penwith Film Society*, a non-profit organisation, screens alternative films – usually foreign ones (not during the summer months).

What?

Adults £6, children and pensioners £4.

How much?

16 Causeway Head, Tel. 01736-363330, www.merlin cinemas.co.uk, www.penwithfilmsociety.co.uk.

Where?

On mild late-summer evenings the *Penwith Film Society*, the Acorn Arts Centre and Penlee House co-present **films in the pleasant ambience of Penlee Park**.

Tip

Cinema magazine

Movie Magic is the magazine of the Cornwall/Devon cinema chain *Merlin Cinemas*, to which the Savoy in Penzance belongs. For a typically commercial in-house magazine, *Movie Magic* shows tangible enthusiasm. There is an emphasis on the editorial section, and it includes a good events calendar for Cornwall, weighted towards music (with Penzance as a separate subheading).

What?

Free of charge.

How much?

Available in the cinema or at www.cornwallmoviemagic.co.uk.

Where?

PENZANCE AS A FILM LOCATION

The area around Penzance is evidently **ideal as a location for films of very differing genres**. Popular motifs: St Michael's Mount, the venerable manor houses, the moor, the cliff-lined bays, villages as if from another age and the urban ambience of Penzance, with its Victorian facades.

- **Twelfth Night** (1996): Perfect setting: in the castle of **St Michael's Mount** – here called 'Orsino's Castle' – three people stubbornly fail to engage in matters of love. The director Trevor Nunn set Shakespeare's amusing and tragic comedy of confusion in the 1920s.
- **Dracula** (1979): St Michael's Mount is chameleonic. In Badham's film version of Bram Stoker's classic the castle on the rocks emerges from the sea as Dracula's Castle one fateful, pitch-black night.
- **Straw Dogs** (1971): Filmed in **Lamorna Cove and St Buryan**. Excellent film starring Dustin Hoffman, about the origin and escalation of violence. Ordinary American citizen moves with his wife to a supposedly calm Cornish village and is there attacked by the villagers – until he wreaks his revenge.
- **Love Story** (1944): A semi-blind pilot and a pianist with heart disease fall in love in Cornwall. For schmaltz of this nature there is no better backdrop than the **Minack Theatre** in the cliffs at Porthcurno, but because of inclement weather during filming the team had to fall back on a not exactly convincing studio model of the open-air theatre.

Rosamunde Pilcher locations

Every Sunday evening German households wonder: Shall we take a look at Cornwall today? Ever since 1993, week after week the German broadcasting company ZDF has been transmitting its own filmings of the novels by the best-selling author Rosamunde Pilcher, who was born in Lelant. It is only through this TV series that many Germans know about the **spectacular Cornish coast, the idyllic fishing villages, the deserted bays, the imposing country houses and the exotic gardens**.

The German films have been sold to 28 countries – a fact that has greatly boosted tourism in Cornwall and continues to do so. In 2002

Rosamunde Pilcher even received the British Tourist Award for her contribution to tourism.

Over 60 Rosamunde Pilcher films have been made since 1993, and many of them are set in Penzance and its environs. **Penzance** itself is the secret capital of 'Pilcher country', as **in the novels it is the town mentioned most frequently**. Thus Penzance acts as the pivotal und focal point for the films. Some of the locations:

- **Penzance harbour:** *The Day of the Storm*, the very first Pilcher film from 1993 takes place where the ships lie at anchor.
- **Trengwainton Garden:** A good two miles northwest of Penzance is this subtropical garden paradise, which is used as the setting for the cricket scene at the beginning of the film *The Empty House*.
- **Marazion:** The sweet little town facing St Michael's Mount has already served as a location for several Pilcher films. Large sections of *Voices in Summer* were recorded in the picturesque alleys, and the town also provided the setting for young Dr Wells' practice in the two-parter *Coming Home*.
- **Porthgwarra:** This lonely bay southwest of Porthcurno was to serve as the location for a **romantic nude-bathing scene** for the film *Coming Home*. But this wasn't to be: 57 fishermen got wind of the planned juicy shots and cruised their boots up and down in front of the bay.
- **Land's End:** The charming final sequence of *The Day of the Storm*, which takes place on the large open area below the restaurant, was filmed aerially. In keeping with the title, things were also stormy on board the helicopter, which lacked the usual vibration-free camera attachment, thus the cameraman had to develop a very calm hand.

FILMS ABOUT PENZANCE AND ITS ENVIRONS

A fair number of documentary-makers have taken a shine to the Land's End peninsula and used it for a wide variety of topics. The *South West Film & Television Archive* in Plymouth houses around 110,000 films and video clips on all relevant topics in the southwest from the 20s to the present day. They include amusing little films by amateur film-makers

about their own families on seaside holidays. Various clips can be viewed on the website, and other films can be ordered from the archive.
Information: www.movinghistory.ac.uk/archives/sw.

- **Painting the Warmth of the Sun** (1984): Three-part series on the artists of the *Newlyn School* and the *St Ives School*, including interviews with the artists and their critics.
- **The Gill Collection** (1930–40): The amateur film-maker Major Gill has created important documents of the age: In the 30s he produced **films and clips on many aspects of rural life in West Cornwall**, including mining, fishing, serpentine stone machining, boat-building and much more. In the process he recorded various dialects and regionally varying clothing for posterity.

PIRATES

After the death of his parents Frederic was actually to become a pilot, but his wet nurse had understood 'pirate' and passed the child into the protection of a pirate king.

Thus begins the **world-famous Gilbert & Sullivan musical 'Pirates of Penzance'** – the only work by the successful duo to have its official premiere in New York. This 'comic opera' has been adapted as a film countless times, a particularly successful version being the 1982 film by the director Wilford Leach (NB: Several versions were made in and around 1982 alone!).

The Pirates of Penzance and Pretty Woman

After a visit to the opera *La Traviata* an elderly lady asks 'Pretty Woman' (Julia Roberts): "Did you enjoy the opera, dear?"
Pretty Woman: "Oh, it was so good, I almost peed in my pants."
Elderly lady: "What?"
Edward Lewis (Richard Gere): **"She said she liked it better than Pirates of Penzance."**
Source: DVD Pretty Woman © 2001 Buena Vista Home Entertainment Inc.

Film websites

- **www.rosemarylinks.co.uk/film.htm**: Broad overview of (TV) films set in Cornwall.
- **www.cornwallfilmfestival.com**: Since November 2002 annual festival in Falmouth on Cornish topics and Cornish film-makers.
- **www.cornwallfilm.com**: Insider site for film-makers who choose Cornwall as a location. Information on production companies, locations and the wealth of (financial) support available.

Media

Newspaper

- **The Cornishman**: Weekly newspaper since 1878. For West Cornwall, with an emphasis on Penzance, comes out on Thursdays. Very comprehensive events supplement (about 40 pages!). Costs 80p.

Magazines

- **Inside Cornwall**: Glossy monthly magazine focusing on food, art, lifestyle, events and gardens. £2.50. (The publishing house is in Newlyn.)
- **Cornwall Today**: Magazine for a slightly older target group, featuring many cultural and historical topics, and with an emphasis on wildlife and nature. Lovely photographs. Comes out monthly, £3.50.
- **Cornish World**: A thoroughly Cornish magazine, focusing on topics such as preservation of the Cornish language and culture. Subscribers from over 30 countries. Comes out every other month and costs £3.50.

Radio

- **BBC Radio Cornwall**: The BBC's local radio station in Cornwall, providing regional events calendar and good background reports. Quite a lot on surfing. On 95.2/103.9 FM.
- **Pirate FM**: This is the only private radio station in Cornwall, and it has been transmitting since 1992.

Music from the 70s to the present day, events calendar several times a day. On 102.2/102.8 FM.

Websites
- **www.thisiscornwall.co.uk/whatson**: Good online events calendar of the weekly paper *The Cornishman*, with all the important categories.
- **www.tripadvisor.com**: Independent assessment of hotels by visitors. Currently 300 reviews of different places to stay in Penzance. Very helpful, as everything is laid bare.
- **www.penzance.co.uk**: This website is sponsored by the local chamber of commerce, and evidently wants to stimulate trade in the town. Overview of sights in the region and current weather forecast for Penzance.

- See chapter 'Accommodation' for websites featuring hotels/B&Bs in Penzance and surroundings.

Tip
The TIC brings out the **free monthly flyer 'What's On in West Cornwall'**. Ask for it!

Shopping

PRESENTS
The Painted Bird

The very appearance of this bright little corner shop
with its colourful mosaic-like windows catches your
eye. At least as appealing are the many small items such
as notebooks, letter paper, purses, glasses and shawls
– mostly from the region, e.g. tasteful ceramic goods
from the *Fish Pye Pottery* in St Ives, plus selected items
from France, Holland and further afield. Our favourite:
the beautiful *Lucy Art* cards. — What?

Mon–Sat 9.30am–5.30pm. — When?

41 Market Jew Street (on the right-hand side coming up
from the station), Tel. 01736-366714, www.thepainted
bird.co.uk. — Where?

Mount's Bay Trading

Everything under the sun. This big shop is packed to the
hilt with pretty things, ranging from florally decorated
home accessories and all sorts of nice bits and bobs,
which just manage to steer clear of being useless knick-
knacks, through to furniture and clothes (for both sex-
es). All in a sort of modern country style. — What?

Mon–Sat 9.30am–5.30pm, in the summer open from
9am. — When?

8/9 Causewayhead, Tel. 01736-362829. — Where?

Just Cornish

Not quick enough to take a snap at sunrise in Mousehole? No problem, as there are wonderful photos here.
Also books on Cornish topics, prints and postcards, folk
music and Cornish chilli sauce. Everything – even the
jams and chutneys – somehow with an arty touch. — What?

When?   Mon–Fri 9.30am–5.20pm.
Where?   65 Causewayhead, Tel. 01736-331616, www.justcornish.
         co.uk.

Top 3 Penzance souvenirs

- A **hand-made bag by the Newlyn designer Poppy Treffry** and
  other charming frippery (purses, egg-warmers, buttons). From *Kit*
  (Albert Street) or direct from www.poppytreffry.co.uk.
- Preserves by Wendy and Barrie Sisley from Penzance. The **black-
  berry & apple jam with clotted cream** is delicious, likewise the
  Cornish chutney with apples, onions, raisins and Cornish ale.
  Cheers! Or rather, Bon appétit! Available from *Just Cornish* (Causewayhead) and *The Deli* (Market Place), and at www.sisleyscornish
  preserves.com.
- A **Sue Lewington book with heart-rendingly beautiful drawings** featuring Cornish motifs (not kitschy!). Available in the bookshops.

CLOTHES
Kit

What?   Selected items made by small labels, ranging from *Mink
         Bikini* (pretty smart) to *Paul Frank* (pretty amusing).
         Someone here obviously has a good feel for the rare
         combination of individuality and practicality. Our high-
         light is the sweet little bags by Poppy Treffry, a New-
         lyn designer.
When?   Mon–Sat 10am–5pm.
Where?   5a Albert Street (two minutes from the station), Tel.
         01736-333903.

Fishboy

What?   Own-label T-shirts: very cool and really good prints. Plus
         streetwear by other designers, e.g. *Chunk or Stussy*.

Mon–Sat 11am–6pm, sometimes also Sundays. **When?**
64 Chapel Street, Tel. 01736-331846, www.fishboypz. **Where?**
co.uk.

Cargo

Shopping trip for grannies and teenage granddaughters **What?**
alike. You suddenly realise that you don't need a special
occasion to buy chic clothes – and certainly not for our
favourite jewellery by *Pilgrim*.
Mon–Sat 10am–5.30pm. **When?**
84 Market Jew Street, Tel. 01736-331044, www.cargo **Where?**
clothing.com.

- Bookshops in the chapter 'Literature' **More**
- Artists' requisites in chapter 'Art' **shopping**
- Music and musical instruments in chapter 'Music'
- Food shopping/delis in the chapter 'Food'

Going out

It is not just in the daytime that Penzance forms a sort of node for West Cornwall. When everywhere is shutting up shop for the day in the villages, nightlife enthusiasts go into town. **Penzance's nightlife caters for many different tastes.** Pub-goers will get their money's worth in one of the numerous and mostly pleasant traditional pubs. If you like sipping cocktails and a Mediterranean bar atmosphere you'll find *Blue Snappa*, *Cocos* (see under 'Restaurants') and *Renaissance* (see 'Cafés') just the ticket. Boppers will go to one of the two clubs. For anyone who can't stand any more mainstream music, Penzance has two great alternatives: the *Groove Lounge* in the Arts Club or live music in the *Studio Bar* (see chapter 'Music').

PUBS
Smugglers' nest
Turks Head

What?   This, the oldest pub in Penzance, dates from 1233, and is very cosy and well known for its excellent food. Here you can still find the entrance to a secret tunnel, through which alcohol used to be smuggled from the harbour to the bar. A good selection of real ales, a leafy beer garden and fresh local fish in the homely restaurant corner. The hot sticky toffee pudding is absolute nectar – and the portions are huge!

How much?   Mains £7.50 to £16 (fillet steak). Beer £2.45 a pint.

When?   Mon–Sat 11am–3pm and 5.30–11pm, Sun 12–3pm and 5.30–10.30pm. Lunch 11am–2.30pm, Sun from 12pm; evening meals 6–10pm.

Where?   19 Chapel Street, Tel. 01736-363093, www.turkshead penzance.co.uk.

Welcome on board

Admiral Benbow

You almost expect the floor to sway when you enter the smugglers' bar with all its nooks and crannies. Everything here is like on a ship: ships' wheels instead of window frames, brightly coloured figureheads, parts of wrecks – wonderful in its exaggeration. Real ales and good food. Tip: Upstairs there are fewer tourists and you get a marvellous panoramic view of Mount's Bay. And incidentally, the opening scene of Robert Louis Stevenson's 'Treasure Island' is set in the Admiral Benbow. Mains £9 to £14. Beer £2.20 a pint.

Mon–Sat 11am–11pm, Sun 12–10.30pm. Food 12.30–2.30pm and 5.30–9.30pm.

46 Chapel Street, Tel. 01736-363448.

What?

How much?
When?

Where?

A good solid local

Crown Inn

What? This friendly little corner pub is a meeting place for relaxed people of all ages. Tourists seldom find their way here, as the pub – though very central – is a bit hidden away. There's good beer and delicious home-made food. Tuesday is Quiz Night.

How much? Beer £2.40 a pint, mains £5.50 to £14.

When? Mon–Thur 12pm-midnight, Fri/Sat half an hour longer.

Where? Victoria Square (three minutes from the station), Tel. 01736-351070.

BAR

Night & Day

Blue Snappa

What? Classy cocktails and a trendy atmosphere, with wooden floors, a long Cornish granite bar and a good selection of wine and tapas. And for early risers whose stomach can take it, Blue Snappa's breakfast should not be missed – according to *The Cornishman* the best in Cornwall.

How much? Large wine £3.95, large plate of tapas £10.25

When? Mon–Thur 9.30am-11pm, Fri/Sat 9.30am-1am, Sun 10.30am–5pm (high season until 11pm). Breakfast until 11.30am.

Where? 35 Market Place, Tel. 01736-363352, www.bluesnappa. com.

CLUBS

It's scandalous - Penzance's best club has just closed! *Bosun's Locker* on the harbour really rocked, and at least some of the music was outside the mainstream. The alternatives are meagre, especially if charts, house and hip-hop are not your favourites. Luckily there's the Arts Club with its *Groove Lounge*.

Not to be missed
Groove Lounge
In the unique living room atmosphere of the Arts Club,   **What?**
every two weeks DJs spoil their guests with funk, soul,
jazz and Latin rarities (see playlist on the net). Between
the candelabra and the fireplace a really special party
atmosphere always develops. Groove Lounge has now
become something of an own brand in Penzance, and
is sometimes also booked for the Acorn Theatre and
Club 2K.

Entry £5.   **How much?**

Every other Friday from 8.30pm (it doesn't get full un-   **When?**
til later, but it's really nice having a drink here beforehand).

Arts Club, Chapel House, Chapel Street, Tel. 01736-   **Where?**
367416, www.groovelounge.co.uk.

Party alarm
Club 2K
Like your first party at home with coloured tissue paper   **What?**
atmospherically stuck to the ceiling spotlights. At Club
2K they're more professional, and proud of their clev-
er lighting system, but the pink, blue and green party
light is still dreadful. OK, it's a matter of taste. For fans
of hip-hop and house and for people who like knock-
ing it back, the 'first and last nightclub in the country'
is the place to go. Fri: Hip-Hop/R'n'B/House; Sat: Hip-
Hop with notorious local DJs; Sun: R'n'B/Charts/Dance
Classics. Top-guest DJs/Live Acts.

Entry £2–£6 depending on the event.   **How much?**

Open Tue/Thur–Sun from 10pm.   **When?**

Branwell's Mill, straight opposite the station. Tel. 01736-   **Where?**
331211, www.club2k.co.uk.

For fun-seekers

Barn Club

What?
: The pub's motto 'Anything goes' is to be taken literally. People are pulled and picked up here like nobody's business, thus the club is known to locals as the 'meat market'. Under disco lights there's wall-to-wall chart music, sometimes going back into the 80s. You're here to have fun at all costs!

How much?
: Entry £2–£6, depending on the evening. Drink promos.

When?
: Open three evenings a week from 10.30pm: Tue until 2am, Fri 3am, Sat 3.30am.

Where?
: Eastern Green, on the Tesco roundabout on the A30 just outside Penzance. Tel. 01736-365754, www.barnclub.com.

Gardens

It's green everywhere! In every corner of the town you can find small and large oases of vegetation, and palms and other exotic plants grow between the houses. Even in winter there are brightly coloured flowers in Penzance. The influence of the Gulf Stream ensures a mild climate, and **everything seems to be green and in flower for longer than anywhere else in the country**.

Meditative
Morrab Gardens
Where there was once a sand dune that dropped away to the coast, ever since 1889 there has been a **subtropical garden paradise**. Right in the middle of Penzance plants such as Cornish palm, bamboo and aloe vera flourish – plants which actually originate from the Mediterranean, if not from even warmer climes. The benches around the fountain are the best place for reflection (the even splashing creates a meditative atmosphere) or for enjoying a Cornish pasty in peace and quiet. — What?

From sunrise to sunset, depending on the whim of the security staff. — When?

Free. — How much?

Access either from the lower part of Morrab Road or from a turning off Parade Street. www.morrablibrary.co.uk — Where?

Glorious green
Penlee Memorial Park
Behind Penlee House Museum lies the park, with its stock of old trees, tennis courts, pond, playground and open-air theatre. The separate **Garden of Remembrance** is particularly beautiful; it is **an oasis of calm** that is an — What?

excellent place to retreat to with a book. The subtropical plants flower here nearly all year round.

When? The main park opens early in the morning and closes at dusk. Garden of Remembrance 9am–4pm.

How much? Free.

Where? Entry either from the Morrab Road side or from the Trewithen Road side. www.penleehouse.org.uk.

TIPS ON GARDEN TRIPS

It isn't easy making a choice, as in the immediate vicinity of Penzance alone (approx. as far as Helston to the east) there are twelve wonderful gardens and large areas encompassing nurseries and tree nurseries.

Information: If you want a complete overview, the TIC stocks the 'Cornwall Gardens Guide' and the leaflet 'Great Gardens of Cornwall' – both free. It's also a good idea to look on the Internet: www.gardensofcornwall. com and www.greatgardensofcornwall.co.uk.

Noah's Ark
Trengwainton Garden

What? Exotic and dreamy garden on the edge of Penzance that is famed for its **magnificent magnolias**. A stream flows romantically through the garden, and many rare plants flourish in the protected surroundings. **Glorious views** of St Michael's Mount and as far as The Lizard from a raised terrace. Of particular interest is the walled garden with its strangely sloping beds – said to be based on the structure of Noah's Ark. The gigantic tree ferns make it seem like a primeval forest. The café offers delicious home-made cakes, sandwiches and savoury dishes.

When? Mid–February to early November, Sun–Thur 10am–5pm.

How much? £5.20. Children (6–16) £2.60, family and group tickets available. NB: If you come by public transport, on foot or by bike it costs less.

Two miles northwest of Penzance via Heamoor towards Madron, or by No. 17 bus towards St Just (about 15 min.). Cycle- and footpaths also lead straight to the garden. Tel. 01736-363148, www.nationaltrust.org.uk.

Where?

A machete instead of a kiss – the Sleeping Beauty lives!

Lost Gardens of Heligan

Enchanted garden of the Tremayne family, who resided here for 400 years. 22 gardeners used to keep the 32 hectares in shape, but after WW1 the garden became increasingly overgrown. Rescue came in 1990 in the form of the Dutch **rock musician Tim Smit**, botanist und friend of the Heligan heir John Willis. Beneath the stinging nettles and ivy Smit found a botanic treasure trove and **brought the 'lost gardens' back to life**. This reconstruction of the original gardens now offers an enchanted primeval forest complete with bamboos and palms, an Italian garden with giant sized courgettes and a lost valley.

What?

March–Oct daily 10am–6pm (entry until 4.30pm), Nov–Feb daily 10am–5pm (entry until 3.30pm).

When?

£8.50, OAPs £7.50, children (5–16) £5, under-5s free of charge. Family and group tickets available.

How much?

Near St Austell, from where you should take the B3273 towards Mevagissey then follow the signs to Heligan. By public transport: to St Austell by train (55 min.), then about 35 min. by *First* bus No. 25 or *Western Greyhound* bus No. 526. Tel. 01726-845100, www.heligan.com.

Where?

Rainy day programme

Eden Project

The **biggest greenhouses in the world** proudly project from the Cornish soil like some kind of futuristic gi-

What?

ant honeycomb. The Eden millennium project was re-alised for £76m in 2001, to a design by the star architect Nicholas Grimshaw. Eden has over a million plants, and the **eight enormous greenhouses represent the earth's various climate zones**. Eleven double-decker buses stacked on top of each other or the entire Tower of London would fit into the biggest of the greenhouses. Every year 1.25 million visitors experience the link between nature and technology here (though the vast amounts of electricity consumed do not come from alternative sources!).

When? April–Oct 9am–6pm (entry until 4.30pm), Nov–March 10am–4.30pm (entry until 3pm).

How much? £14, OAPs £10, students £7, children (5–18) £5, under-5s free of charge. Reductions for groups of ten or more to be booked in advance.

Where? Four miles from St Austell. Special buses from St Austell station. By car A30 to Innis Downs roundabout, then follow the signs. 01726-811911, www.edenproject.com.

The Eden Project

Beach

Penzance has three small town beaches, which are ideal for a breath of fresh air now and again. In the vicinity of Penzance there are a wealth of the small sandy bays flanked by cliffs that are typical for Cornwall. They are easily reached by bus or car, and you can find **gems of beaches that would put the Caribbean to shame.** The individual locations are so different that you'd think nature had consciously provided something for every taste.

FOR SURFERS
Gwenver Beach

Top surfing beach at the western tip of Cornwall. **One of the most exposed beaches in Great Britain.** Spectacular waves and strong currents, so not really suitable for beginners. **Beautiful location** framed by mysterious green cliffs, and in good weather you can see straight to the Isles of Scilly. Gwenver or Gwynver, as it is sometimes known here, is far less busy than the neighbouring Sennen Cove. Lifeguards from May to the end of September, daily 10am–6pm. The best surfing here is at low tide.

waiting for the perfect wave

Getting there: Head towards Land's End on the A30, then at the chapel just before Sennen turn right towards *Tregiffian Farm*. From the cliff car park 10-15 min. on foot down to the beach on a worn path. About 45 min. to Sennen Cove by No. 1 *First* bus or No. 345 *Sunset* Land's End link bus, and from there about 25 min. along the coast path to Gwenver Beach.

Further surfing beaches
- **Sennen Cove:** Magnificent, somewhat more protected bay, though huge waves here too. Busier than Gwenver, with lots of families, bodyboarders and beginner surfers. Surf school (www.sennensurfing centre.com).
- **Porthmeor Beach** (St Ives): Totally surf-oriented, with surf school, board hire and lifeguards. High waves without the frenzy of Newquay. Better for beginners than Gwenver.
- **Gwithian Beach** (Hayle): Three miles of sandy beach with picturesque dune backdrop. Ideal surfing conditions.

Surfing weather
- **Cornish Coast High & Low Tide Times** *(Holidaymaker Publications)*: Little yellow booklet showing high/low tides and sunrise/sunset for all coastal locations in Cornwall for a year. £1.20 in the bookshops.
- **www.a1surf.com:** Current information on wind and weather for all surfing beaches in Cornwall, plus tide table.
- **Surfcall:** Surfing conditions in the southwest on Tel. 09068-360360.

FOR WINDSURFERS
Marazion Beach and Long Rock
THE place in Cornwall for windsurfing, **right in front of the imposing St Michael's Mount**, which rises majestically out of the water. International windsurfing championships take place here at Easter *(South West Coup)*, and kiteboarding is on the ascendant too. Mount's Bay is held to be one of the ten most beautiful bays on the world, though the beach is a bit stony, and it can be pretty painful if you're barefoot. Windsurfing shop und repair service *(Lodey Sails)* on site.

Getting there: From Penzance follow the coast eastwards, and park right next to the beach, which is separated off by an unattractive concrete wall. 10 min. on the No. 2 or No. 17B *First* bus or the No. 340 *Sunset* bus.

windsurfing in
Mount's Bay

FOR ROMANTICS
Nanjizal

Wonderfully isolated, with a backdrop whose many caves are **reminiscent of Enid Blyton's 'The Famous Five on a Treasure Island'**. Just to the southeast of Land's End is this jewel of a bay, which even on a hot July day can be empty. In the 60s Nanjizal was an extremely popular beach, but big storms then simply swept away the sand, which is now gradually building up again. Depending on the sea's mood, stones and sand dominate alternately; swimming in the protection of the bay is safe. Also a favourite spot for twitchers.

Getting there: Leave your car in the lay-by near Trevescan on the B3315, then 20 min. by foot across the fields towards the coast. Or from the coastal path, coming either from Land's End or Porthgwarra (both a good half hour). About 50 min. on the No. 1 or No. 345 bus.

Further beaches for romantics:

- **Porthchapel Beach**: Beautiful bay – next one along from Porthcurno. Beware: it's quite a climb down. Best at low tide.
- **Portheras Cove**: Lonely bay on one of the wildest sections of the Cornish coast between Pendeen and Morvah. Seals can often be seen in the water. Park at Pendeen Lighthouse.

FOR FAMILIES
Praa Sands

Between Penzance and Helston is Praa Sands (pron. 'Pray'), a favourite holiday spot. A mile long **fine sandy beach** with green dunes behind it slopes **gradually into the sea**, and is thus ideal for children to paddle in. At the northern end of the beach the headland Hoe Point offers perfect protection against westerly winds. Praa Sands has quite high waves, making it ideal for surfers too. Lifeguards on duty. Fantastic sunset because of the beach's southwesterly orientation, e.g. from the *Sandbar*'s terrace.

Getting there: By car on the A394 towards Helston or on the No. 2 bus from Penzance (25 min.), alighting at Praa Sands Post Office.

Further family beaches
- **Porthminster Beach** (St Ives): Protected by St Ives Bay, the sea is usually calm and free of waves. Minigolf course.
- **Carbis Bay Beach**: Long sandy beach and calm sea.
- **Sennen**: Glorious sandy beach, targeted at families with children.
- **Porthcurno**: Perfect family beach. Excellent opportunities for playing beside a small stream at the top of the beach.

FOR NUDISTS
Pedn Vounder
A bay of such beauty as to make you almost giddy with joy. **Crystal-clear water, golden sand, embedded in a spectacular rocky landscape.** At the eastern end of the unofficial nudist beach the breathtaking cliffs of Treryn Dinas stretch far out into the sea, and at the top you can make out the famous Logan Rock – a 70-tonne granite rock that used to be balanced in such a way that it rocked if you gave it a good push. Uninterrupted feeling of paradise because of the lack of beach cafés etc. (as an alternative: *The Logan Rock Inn* in Treen). NB: Beach only exists at low tide.
Getting there: By car either to Treen (½ mile north of the beach), then 10 min. by foot past the campsite to the coast path, followed by a bit of rock-climbing down to the bay, or park in Porthcurno (½ mile to the west). 30 min. by No. 1 bus from Penzance to Treen, or 36 min. by the same bus to Porthcurno. The No. 345 also goes to both places.

FOR DOG OWNERS
Most beaches in Cornwall ban dogs from Easter to 1st October, but on some sections of beaches and bays dogs can rush around to their heart's content all year round. They include:
- **Eastern Green**: Small town beach at the eastern end of Penzance behind the bus station.
- **Long Rock**: The extension of Eastern Green towards Marazion (in Marazion itself dogs have to leave the beach again).

- **Wherrytown**: Section of beach at the western end of the promenade just before Newlyn (not the promenade beach itself).
- **Sandy Cove/Roskilly/Salt Ponds**: All three around Mousehole (dogs are not allowed on the harbour beach in Mousehole).
- On **Pedn Vounder/Nanjizal/Gwenver** and on **all the beaches around St Just und Cape Cornwall** dogs are allowed all year round.

FOR EVERYONE
Porthcurno Beach
The Caribbean definitely cannot compete with this. Porthcurno Bay is an extra special feast for the eyes: ultra-turquoise water, soft golden sand, framed by perfectly curved cliffs. As if that were not enough beauty, the unique open-air **Minack Theatre sits in solitary splendour above the beach**, hewn into the rugged cliffs. The beach is protected from the wind by the steep rock faces on both sides, and is a suntrap. Unfortunately it's sometimes pretty busy here, but the setting amply makes up for this.

Getting there: Seven miles southwest of Penzance on the B3315 to Porthcurno. Pay car park in the village (come early, as it fills up relatively quickly!). Just under 40 min. to Porthcurno by No. 1 or No. 345 bus.

Activities

WALKING
Lamorna Cove – Mousehole – Merry Maidens
Length: 8 miles, circular route.

Duration: about 5 hours (without stop in Mousehole).

Getting there: No. 345 bus from Penzance to The Wink in Lamorna (30 min.) or No. 1/1A/101 bus to the Lamorna Turning stop (20 min.), the turn-off from the B3315 just before Lamorna. Parking down at Lamorna Cove is fairly expensive, and if you exceed your time limit even marginally you'll get clamped. So it's better to leave your car outside Lamorna and walk for a few minutes.

Mousehole is a possible starting point instead of Lamorna. **Depending how you feel, you can shorten the route** by leaving out either Mousehole or the Merry Maidens.

Tip

Over the cliffs to Mousehole

The coast path starts at Lamorna Cove and goes east (with the sea on your right). The path is wide to start with, and you can clearly see what's ahead. Often **close to the cliff edge**, you have to clamber over lumps of rock and finally granite steps, ascending evenly to **Carn-du** headland. Turn round and enjoy the view of Lamorna Cove and over to Tater-du Lighthouse.

Granite steps now lead downwards, and a **breathtaking backdrop** opens out before you, with St Michael's Mount on the left and Lizard Point over to the right. On sunny days you can even make out the

twinkling of the Goonhilly satellite dishes on **The Lizard**. On a fairly even stretch the coast path winds along the **Kemyel cliffs** and round the chasm of **Zawn Organ**. After about 35 minutes' hike the path goes through a sort of **sylvan tunnel (Kemyel Crease Nature Reserve)** before descending a few steps to **Slinke Dean stream**. From there the stepped coast path winds up- and downhill – though mostly steeply uphill! – to **Penzer Point**. At the top there's a coastguard lookout and, thank goodness, a welcome bench for a quick breather.

After about an hour you'll reach the 'Lamorna Inland Route' turn-off. If you just want to walk, and take in Mousehole on another occasion (don't miss it, though!), turn left and head back to Lamorna. Otherwise continue along the coast past **Point Spaniard**. The Spanish landed here in 1595 and devastated Penzance, Newlyn, Paul and Mousehole. Amble downhill into the atmospheric village of **Mousehole**. (See chapter 'Excursions' regarding exploration of the village.)

Return route to Lamorna across idyllic meadows and fields

First go up the steep road out of Mousehole. When you've got to the top, turn left and follow the path across the fields, past two lone, towering megaliths (standing stones) to **Kemyel Drea**, and then through a dubiously-smelling dairy farm. After the tiny hamlet **Kemyel Crease** come meadows (of cows) and stiles to be climbed over, before you get to **Kemyel Wartha**, from where a woodland path leads down to Lamorna Cove. You pass through a **disused quarry**, which supplied the stones for London Bridge and Penzance's Market House. Well-earned refreshment in the *Lamorna Cove Café*.

To the Merry Maidens

You once again start at Lamorna Cove, but this time going west past the café to the coast path. Watch out, as right from the start the path here goes very close to the crumbling stony edge of the cliffs. At the next headland, **Lamorna Point**, there is a weather-beaten Celtic cross in memory of a certain 'Emma' who lost her life here in a shipping accident in the 19th century. The gleaming white **Tater-du Lighthouse** is reached via steps after about half an hour. Leave Tater-du on your left, pass through two green gates and at the next fork keep to the right, heading inland.

Simply follow the path through the fields, past Tregiffian Farm, until you reach a big road, then turn right. Immediately on the right-hand side of the road is the early-Bronze-Age **Tregiffian Burial Chamber**, which is at least 4,000 years old. It is largely hidden under a hill, but the entrance has been uncovered and a stone with a so-called cup-and-ring marking serves as a barrier. This stone is actually a copy, the original being in Truro's *Royal Cornwall Museum*.

A few hundred metres further on, an arrow directs you to the right, onto the field where the famous **Merry Maidens stone circle** stands.

Merry Maidens
According to legend the towering Bronze Age stones represent 19 virgins who **on the holy day of Sunday indulged in dancing and were turned to stone as a punishment**.
Cornwall's best-known stone circle is nearly 24 m in diameter. The individual stones are about 1.20 m high and are positioned non-equidistantly (three to four metres apart). Due east there is a big gap between the stones which is assumed to be the astronomically aligned entrance to the cult site.

Leave the Merry Maidens by a stile in the corner of the meadow, follow the path to a further stile, and climb over this to reach the main road. Immediately turn off to the right again, towards *Menwinnion Country House*, and don't be put off by the cul-de-sac sign.

At Menwinnion old people's home you'll come to a **woodland path**. Follow it downhill through a pretty wood, and when you're back on the road turn off to the right and head straight for Lamorna Cove. On the home straight you won't be able to resist rewarding yourself with a **good pint at the atmospheric Wink Inn**, which is crammed to the ceiling with knick-knacks.

Further walks
- **St Michael's Way**: from St Michael's Mount to St Ives on the former pilgrims' route. It's 12½ miles from the south to the north coast of Cornwall. The brochure *St Michael's Way* (£2), complete with maps and a detailed description of the path, is available from the TIC.
- **The South West Coast Path Guide**: brought out by the *South West Coast Path Association* and updated annually, including detailed descriptions of paths, tide tables and timetables, £9.50. Tel. 01752-896237, www.swcp.org.uk.

SWIMMING
In the sea yet not in the sea
Jubilee Pool

Right on the rocky coast between the harbour and the promenade is this impressive and recently fully modernised Art Deco lido from the 30s. It is filled with (chlorinated) sea water taken directly from the adjacent sea, and even has tides, though water is pumped in or out to compensate for them. A unique pool (though it can be pretty cold, especially at the beginning of the season) thanks to the **incomparable backdrop of St Michael's Mount** and passing ships. Café on a terrace overlooking the pool. — **What?**

Daily 11am–7pm from Whitsun to September. — **When?**

£3.85. Junior bathers £2.75. After 5pm half price. Non-swimming guests £1.30. — **How much?**

Battery Road, Tel. 01736-369224, www.jubileepool.co.uk. — **Where?**

CYCLING

The environs of Penzance are ideal for cycle trips with sea views. The 25-mile Route 3 of the *National Cycle Network*, also called the 'First and Last Trail', takes you on beautifully situated cycle tracks, roads and paths from Land's End via Sennen, the Merry Maidens, Lamorna, Mousehole, Penzance and Marazion to Hayle.

Bicycle hire
Cycle Centre

How much?	£10 a day (various types of bicycle), but cheaper if you hire for 5 or 7 days.
When?	Mon–Sat 9am–5.30pm.
Where?	1 New Street, Tel. 01736-351671, www.cornwallcyclecentre.co.uk.

Guided mountain-bike tours
Mobius Bike Trails

What?	From fun hobby cycling through to technically advanced trails featuring jumps and extremely steep sections. This friendly and professional provider of mountain-bike tours uses experienced guides, who are constantly finding hidden paths and know how to enjoy the Cornish landscape to the full. Mobius also offers kite surfing.
How much?	Half day (2–3 hrs) £25, whole day £50 per person including mountain bike, helmet, gloves, water bottles and full liability insurance.
Where?	In Marazion, by the Follyfields car park opposite St Michael's Mount. Tel. 01637-831383, www.mobiusonline.co.uk.

RIDING
Penhalwyn Trekking Centre
Rides through the moors, past historic sites, individually or in groups. Half-day or whole-day rides also possible, all levels and all ages. Book in advance.

£15/hr in groups, £30/hr individual tuition.

In Halsetown, on the B3311 towards St Ives. Tel. 01736-796461.

What?

How much?
Where?

Old Mill Stables
Riding stables since 1962. Beginners and advanced riders of all ages can ride through moors, woods and fields. Special half-hour courses for children (5–6 years). Maximum weight 80 kg, riding hats for hire free of charge. Ring in advance.

£15 for about an hour in groups, £25/hr individual tuition.

On the A30 towards Camborne, Lelant Downs, near Hayle, opposite *St Ives Holiday Village*. Tel. 01736-753045.

What?

How much?

Where?

BOAT TRIPS
With the wind in your hair and a lobster in your hand
Mermaid
Change of perspective: see the rugged coast from the sea whilst hauling a lobster from the water. Is there anything nicer than gliding through the open sea on a sunny day, past picturesque villages, and close to St Michael's Mount, seals, dolphins and fantastic bird life? This very friendly family company with its Cornish skippers and their many insider stories offers both easy-going boat excursions and exciting fishing trips.

Information hut open daily 10am–5pm (Easter to September).

What?

When?

How much?	2 hrs of mackerel fishing £12, 6- to 8-year-olds £8, under-sixes £2 (you can take the whole of your catch home with you!). Similar prices for boat trips.
Where?	Booking at the little wooden hut by Ross Bridge or on Tel. 07901-731201, www.cornwallboattrips.com.

Nabbed between two trips to sea
Adrian Thomas, proprietor of Mermaid – Fishing Trips & Coastal Cruises

What trip is suitable for whom? "Mackerel fishing is great for **children**, because they can take part, but we also offer angling trips for **professionals**. The 'Minack Theatre Cruise' is calm and very romantic, and thus highly suitable for **couples**. The trip to the seal cove is particularly popular with all and sundry."

Adrian is quite a **sea dog**. Ever since the age of 15 he has spent most of his time at sea, including jobs on ferries and 28 years' work for *Trinity House*. Since 2003 he and his wife Vanessa, who looks after the information hut, have run 'Mermaid'.

Excursions

Penzance Tourist Information Centre stocks **free leaflets on all the nearby localities** ('Discover ...'), describing pleasant 30- to 60-minute circular routes.

Tip

GUIDED TOURS

On the road with Crocodile Dundee

Harry Safari

Harry's 'untouristy' tours are highly recommendable. Harry is a real one-off. He is acquainted with every nook and cranny of the area, knows every story and every plant, wears crocodile teeth on his hat and **takes travellers to places they would never find on their own**. If you want to experience the real Cornwall you must try Harry.

What?

Whenever there's a group of two to eight people, nearly every day of the summer.

When?

£20 for a 4-hour tour (they often last 5 hours. Harry: *"There's simply too much to see."*). All day £30 (approx. 9.30am–4.30pm). If you don't enjoy it you won't have to pay (though this has never happened!).

How much?

Information and booking at the Tourist Information Centre or with Harry in person, Tel. 08456-445940, www.harrysafari.com.

Where?

Through the Wild West with ...
... Harry Glasson alias Safari,
provider of tours for individualists

How did you become Harry Safari? "I used to play a lot of music in pubs, and often got chatting to tourists – I was horrified that so many people come here on holiday and see nothing of the proper Cornwall." A conversation with the TIC, and the alternative tour concept was born.

What is the real Cornwall for you? "Apple pie with clotted cream. And the cliffs, especially the area between St Ives and St Just."

Do your tours take in Land's End or the Merry Maidens? In winter, if at all. Otherwise you've got coach-loads of 150 people there. It takes away the ambience. Treen stone circle near Zennor is far more impressive, but nobody knows about it because there's no road going there.

And lastly, why do you sound like an American, Harry? "That's the Cornish dialect. If an actor is to play a Cornishman, he's simply told to pronounce his vowels and Rs in a typical American accent."

MARAZION

The town of Marazion is often equated with its main attraction, **St Michael's Mount**. But **Cornwall's oldest town** – with its cute cottages, its many galleries and its nice cafés – is certainly worth seeing in its own right. And the rocky, castle-topped islet cloaked in green, which seems to rise mysteriously from the sea, is a constant visual magnet.

Getting there A30 eastbound to the roundabout, right-hand exit onto the A394, signposted. Car park right by the beach. No. 2/2A/2B or 301 bus in 10 min.

It's nicer to **walk to Marazion** (takes nearly an hour). Cross the bus station and follow the 'Cycle Trail' sign. For the first few minutes the trail follows the railways tracks, without any direct sea view, but then the choice is yours: you can either stay on the cycle path or you can go down onto the beach. You admittedly have the road and the railway behind you all the way, but the constant view of St Michael's Mount easily makes up for this. The nearer you get to Marazion the more beautiful the beach and surroundings.

Cutty Sark Bar: pub with very good food – try the prawn salad. On the Square.

Pub/Food

At the **Mount Haven Hotel** – an oasis of relaxation with views of the castle on the rock. At the eastern end of the town (see chapter ‚Accommodation').

Accommodation

Living like lords
St Michael's Mount
About 400 m off the Cornish coast the English twin of France's Norman monastery Mont Saint Michel rises proudly from its granite base. In 1050 the Benedic-

What?

tine monks were bequeathed this rocky islet, where they erected the counterpart of their abbey in France. It has since become a pilgrimage station on the Way of St James to Santiago de Compostela. It later became a fort, and latterly a private dwelling. Beautiful rock garden.

When?   Castle: April–Oct, Mon–Fri and Sun; Garden: May/June Mon–Fri, July–Oct Thur and Fri only. Always 10.30am–5.30pm (last entry 4.45pm).

How much?   Castle: £6.40, children £3.20. Garden: £3, children £1. Family and group tickets. Boat crossing at high tide £1.20.

Where?   From Marazion walk over the causeway at low tide (15 min.), or take the boat at high tide. Tel. 01736-710507, www.stmichaelsmount.co.uk.

NEWLYN

Newlyn is big on fish and art. In terms of size this, **the most important fishing harbour in Cornwall** and one of the richest in Great Britain, is surprisingly understated. The circular route described in the leaflet 'Discover Newlyn' (available from the TIC) is strongly recommended, as you might otherwise fall prey to the belief that Newlyn comprises a single through road. In reality **a tangle of charming alleys wind up- and downhill.**

In around 1900 Newlyn was an **important artists' colony** that started the English plein-air movement. There are still a lot of artists, studios and galleries here, the most important being *Newlyn Art Gallery* (see details in the chapter 'Art').

NB: Ever since 1915 all altitudes in Great Britain have been based on the sea level at Newlyn. The unprepossessing building on the harbour's south pier, next to the lighthouse, houses the measuring station.

Joins on to the west of Penzance. Just amble down the promenade and you'll hit *Newlyn Art Gallery* and the harbour.

Getting there

Fish: **The Smugglers**, good fish restaurant with view of the harbour, 12 14 Fore Street.

Food

Meaderies are typical of the region, **Newlyn Meadery** being the nicest. Rustic ambience, menu big on meat, mediaeval decor and costumes. You eat the chicken with your fingers and rinse it down with Cornish mead, a honey-based alcoholic beverage. Fri from 6.30pm, Sat from 6pm and Sun from 6.30pm – come early, otherwise you'll really have to queue.

Galleries **Newlyn Art Gallery**, on the road to Penzance, and **Badcocks Gallery**, The Strand, show high-quality contemporary art from Cornwall (more detailed information in the chapter 'Art')

MOUSEHOLE

Wherever you look, the views are like picture postcards. A picturesque harbour, florally decorated fishermen's houses bowing over in the wind and stretching up the hill in a mish-mash of narrow alleys. In the distance St Clement's Isle.

The Welsh poet **Dylan Thomas** (1903–1966), who spent his honeymoon here in 1938, described Mousehole as **'the loveliest village in England'.**

Mousehole (pron. 'Mowzel') used to be an important fishing port, and like Penzance it was completely burnt down by the Spanish during their 1595 attack. The inhabitants fled the village and only one man, by the name of Jenkyn Keigwin, remained and defended his house, which is now the oldest building in the town (above the harbour on Keigwin Place). The southern harbour wall is even older, dating from 400 BC. Mousehole was also the home of **Dolly Pentreath, the last per-**

son with Cornish as her mother tongue. She is said to have died aged 102 in 1777.

This little coastal town has a wealth of shops, craft boutiques, galleries, cafés, restaurants, pubs and places to stay. A good starting point for cliff walks. See the chapter 'Activities' for details of the walk to Lamorna Cove.

No. 5A/6/6A bus in 20 min. By car from Newlyn 2½ miles southwards along the coast.

Getting there

Old Coastguard Hotel: Very popular high-class hotel/restaurant, flooded with light, with fantastic view of the harbour. Parade Street, Tel. 01736-731222, www.oldcoastguard hotel.co.uk.

Accommodation/ Food

Ship Inn: Very atmospheric former fishermen's pub. Good beer und food. Own B&B. South Cliff, right by the harbour.

Pub

Mousehole

Festivals The traditional **Maritime Festival** takes place in Mousehole every other July (see chapter 'Entertainment').

December 23rd is **Tom Bawcock's Eve**, an institutionalised **eating orgy**. During a long period of hunger at Christmas time the fisherman Bawcock put out to sea despite a heavy storm and returned with a huge catch, after having been taken for dead. To celebrate this the pubs – and especially the *Ship Inn* – make Stargazey Pie, with whole fish heads sticking out of the top.

Tweet, tweet
Wild Bird Hospital & Sanctuary

What? Founded in 1928, and every year it patches up and nurses back to health about 1,500 sick or injured birds, then sets them free again. It also permanently houses around 100 birds that are too weak to survive in the wild. After the oil tanker Torrey Canyon ran aground between Land's End and the Isles of Scilly in 1967 over 8,000 birds were de-oiled in a very short time.

When? Daily 9am–4.30pm.

How much? Entry free. Financed by donations, so please be generous.

Where? Raginnis Hill, at the beginning of the inland route to Lamorna. Tel. 01736 731386, www.mouseholebirdhospital.org.uk.

LAMORNA COVE

The tiny port is 4 miles southwest of Mousehole. The path to the cove goes through a luxuriantly wooded valley with ivy-entwined trees, at the end of which **a handful of houses stand planted between the rocks**. The stony coast, which contrasts wonderfully with the deep-turquoise water, is a reminder of Lamorna's **quarry**, in which, up until 1911, granite was quarried for the entire country. Lamorna represents retreat in inspiring surroundings – so it's no wonder that an **eminent artists' colony** formed here in the early 20th century (details on this in the chapter 'Art').

Perfect starting point for **cliff walks**. Also various ancient sites in the immediate vicinity. The chapter 'Activities' describes a walk from Lamorna to the **Merry Maidens stone circle**.

Getting there

No. 345/346 bus to Lamorna The Wink (30 min.) or No. 1/1A/101 bus to the Lamorna Turning stop (20 min.), at the turn-off from the B3315 just before Lamorna. It's best to avoid the car park down in the cove – it's expensive, and if you even marginally exceed the time limit you'll be fined. It's better to cover the short distance on foot.

Accommodation

Luxurious: **The Cove** offers luxury apartments in the relaxed ambience of an exquisite, wellbeing-oriented hotel. Tel. 01736-731411, www.lamornacove.com.
Value for money: B&B in the **Lamorna Pottery** (see below).

Pub

Wink Inn: Lovely old-fashioned pub with curios dangling from the ceiling. The name 'Wink' refers to the common practice in the pub's smuggling days of the landlord winking to his guests to indicate that spirits had come in again. On the winding road leading down to the cove.

Best apple pie in the world
Lamorna Pottery

What?

Pottery and restaurant/café offering delicious apple pie. The atmospheric garden with its old trees and wooden benches is an ideal place to take in the country air whilst enjoying an excellent cream tea or a nice cup of coffee. Ever since 1947 ceramic goods in the colours of

	the Cornish landscape have been made in the former milk factory. Large shop, which sells books on the region as well. Also moderately priced B & B.
When?	Daily 10am–5pm, closed from Christmas to 1st February.
How much?	Apple pie with clotted cream £3.95. Something more substantial £4.00–£10.75 (Newlyn crab). B & B from £18 pppn in attic twin room.
Where?	Coming from Penzance on the B3315 before Lamorna Cove, on the turn-off to St Buryan, Tel. 01736-810330.

Moorland and sea
In the workshop of the **Lamorna potters Linda and Ben Craig**

Amidst a confusion of half-finished vessels, plaster moulds into which the liquid clay is poured, dust masks, fettling tools and kilns we meet the **artistic mother-and-son duo**.

What kind of pottery do you actually make? "Crockery, figures, lamp feet – all hand painted and glazed with the colours typical of the Lamorna Pottery. The **brownish-green** series **represents the Cornish moor**, and the **blue mixed with a little green and white represents the sea**. The famous Lamorna Blue is an old secret formulation."

How long have you worked in the Lamorna Pottery? Linda: "Since April 2006. I had a cream tea here, and one thing led to another. I just **seemed to turn up at the right time**."

Linda immediately brought in her son, an art and sculpture graduate of Kingston University. She herself has worked as a ceramic designer and printmaker for many years.

ST IVES

The town has a **magical power of attraction**. The **light** is **extraordinarily clear** and has always attracted artists. In the early/mid-20th century St Ives was a **prominent artists' colony**. Creative energy really is released by the setting, which features **five beaches**, a picturesque harbour with brightly coloured fishing boats, narrow cobbled alleys, Cornish palms and cliffs. The town also boasts numerous art shops/galleries, and **since 1993 Tate St Ives** (see chapter 'Art'). Can be pretty chock-a-block in summer, but definitely worth a visit.

Getting there

Best by train. Firstly because the parking situation is not exactly relaxed and the traffic coming into town is often stacked up in the summer, and secondly because **the view of St Ives Bay from the train is simply unbeatable**. Lean back and enjoy – sit on the right! Change in St Erth, 20-30 min. all in all.

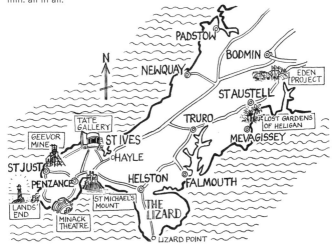

Accommodation	There's one B & B after another here, and most of them are of an excellent standard, e.g. **Treliska**, a nice B & B in Bedford Road – very central.
Pub	**Sloop Inn**: THE meeting place in St Ives. Enchanting harbour pub dating from 1312, good for people-watching, and delicious food.
Café	**Porthgwidden Café**: Hellenic atmosphere on the dazzlingly white terrace overlooking the small and sandy Porthgwidden beach. Good food.

Underground and under the sea

Geevor Tin Mine

UK's biggest preserved tin mine, worked until 1990. Museum and interesting tour of the workings, some of which extend deep below the sea.

What?

Easter–Oct: daily except Sat from 9am, with hourly tours of the workings 10am–4pm. In the winter entry until 3pm, tours at 11am, 1pm and 3pm.

When?

£7.50, OAPs £7, children and students £4.30.

How much?

Pendeen, 7 miles west of Penzance. On the A3071 towards St Just, turn right on the B3318 to Pendeen, signposted. Bus No. 17; let the driver know in advance that you want to get off at Geevor Tin Mine. Tel. 01736-788662, www.geevor.com.

Where?

Don't bother!

Land's End

It could be so lovely breathing in the cool air of the westernmost point of the English mainland. But instead of a wild and romantic experience you'll find a dreadful amusement park: *The Land's End Experience*. What's available outside free of charge is unconvincingly imitated using **artificial background sounds and trivial laser effects**. There are busloads of tourists tripping up over each other, crowding around the souvenirs and queuing to have their photo taken. It's a waste of time! But if you do want to visit Land's End there's nothing to stop you approaching it free of charge along the cliff path. A good half hour from Sennen Cove.

What?

A to Z of Tips for Visitors

Banks   The Banks are all close together. *Barclays* and *Halifax* are in Market Jew Street, *Lloyds TSB, Abbey* and *Bristol & West* are on Market Place, *NatWest* is in Alverton Street and *HSBC* is at Greenmarket. There is an additional *Barclays* in Newlyn, The Strand.

Buses/ Coaches   The big bus station is at the lower end of town opposite the station, and both coaches and regional bus services use it. Bus timetables available from the TIC right next to the bus station, on Tel. 01872-322003 or at www.cornwall.gov.uk/buses. Travel information on Tel. 0870-6082608.

Car parks   Big car park between bus station and harbour, St Anthony's Gardens (opposite the Jubilee Pool), The Greenmarket und Clarence Street (both well placed for Penlee House), Causewayhead and at the western end of the promenade.

Car rentals
- *Tucker's Garage*, Long Rock (on the road to Marazion), Tel. 01736-362980
- *Europcar*, Station Yard, Tel. 01736-368816
- *Enterprise*, The Forecourt, Long Rock, Tel. 01736-332000

Disabilities   The TIC stocks the brochure 'Penzance – A Guide for the Less Abled Visitor'.
Happily, this lists a lot of hotels, restaurants, beaches, museums, taxi firms etc. in and around Penzance that are set up for people with disabilities. If you have any specific questions the *West Cornwall Tourism Office* in St Clare Street will be of assistance, Tel. 01736-362341.

Penzance by no means has a shortage of doctors. Here is a selection:

Doctors/ Dentists/ Vet

GPs
- *Morrab Surgery*, 2 Morrab Road, Tel. 01736-363866
- *Penalverne Surgery*, Penalverne Drive, Tel. 01736-363361

Dentists
- *Dental Surgery*, 5 Alverton Terrace, Tel. 01736-362299
- *Nellist*, 3 Morrab Road, Tel. 01736-363036

Vet
- *Otty & Bruce*, Rosevean House, Coombe Road, Tel. 01736-362215

It can also be helpful to call *National Health Service Direct*, Tel. 0845-4647, who will say what treatments are obtainable where in Cornwall.

999 – Police, fire, ambulance and coastwatch.

Emergency services

The best place is the Arts Club in Chapel Street (see chapter 'Entertainment'). This includes an expressly gay-friendly B&B and a Sunday Gay Night. Outside Penzance in rural Goldsithney there is another nice gay/ lesbian B&B: *Willow Cottage*, West End, Tel. 01736-719062, www.willow-cottage.co.uk. Otherwise see www.gaycornwall.com.

Gay scene

West Cornwall Hospital, St Clare Street, Tel. 01736-874000.

Hospital

- *Library*: Members £2/hr, non-members £3, payment in 15-minute units. 62 Morrab Road
- *Studio Bar*: £1/hr. 40-41 Bread Street, entrance opposite Belgravia Street

Internet

- *Poly Clean*: Surf the net cheaply in the launderette. £1/hr, 50p per ½ hr (minimum). For launderette users the first 15 min. are free (address/opening hours under 'Launderettes')
- *Penzance Computers*: Internet café, £3.75/hr (min. 55p). 36B Market Jew Street (opposite the Wharfside Shopping Centre)
- *Renaissance Café*: Only one computer, £1 per 15 min., plus WiFi, in the Wharfside Centre

Launderettes
- *PolyClean*, 4 East Terrace/corner Leskinnick Street. About £3 per load (self-service). Mon–Thur 9am–5pm, Fri 9am–4pm and Sat 9am–1pm
- *Lee's Launderette*, Taroveor Road/corner Tolver Road. Mon–Sun 8am–10pm, in the winter 8am–8pm (last wash 6.30pm). Price: £7–8.50.

Petrol stations
- *Co-operative*, on the promenade towards Newlyn, Tel. 01736-368639
- *Tolverth Filling Station*, Long Rock, towards Marazion, Tel. 01736-333231

Pharmacies
- *Peasgood's Pharmacy*, 1 Market Place/corner of New Street, Tel. 01736-362110
- *Newlyn Pharmacy*, 5 The Strand, Tel. 01736-362324

Police
Penalverne Drive, close to St John's Hall/Alverton Street, Mon–Sun 8am–6pm, Tel. 08452-777444.

Post Offices
- 113 Market Jew Street, Mon/Wed–Fri 9am–5.30pm, Tue 9.30am–5.30pm, Sat 9am–12.30pm
- Morrab Road, Mon–Fri 8.30am–5.30pm, Sat 9am–12.30pm
- St Clare Street, Mon–Fri 9am–5.30pm, Sat 9am–12.30pm

- The Strand/Newlyn, Mon/Tue 8.45am–5.30pm, Wed–Fri 9am–5.30pm, Sat 9am–12pm

Taxis

Finding a taxi in Penzance should not be a problem. There are always some at the station. A selection:
- *James' Taxis*, Tel. 01736-366166
- *Nippy Cabs*, Tel. 01736-366666
- *Penzance Taxi*, Tel. 01736-366366
- *R-Cars*, Tel. 01736-330564
- Newlyn: *Jonny's Cars*, Tel. 01736-333935 and *Stone's Taxis*, Tel. 01736-363400

Telephones

There are quite a few public phone booths, including by the big car park next to the bus station, at the Jubilee Pool, Morrab Road (at the post office), Clarence Street/corner of Alverton Street und St Clare Street.

Toilets

There are public toilets at the bus station, by the South Pier/harbour, in Jennings Street (near the main post office), opposite St John's Hall, in Clarence Street (at the junction Causewayhead/St Clare Street), next to the casino on the promenade (Alexandra Gardens Playsite) and at the western end of the promenade (opposite *Lidl*).

Tourist Information Centre (TIC)

Right opposite the main station entrance. Station Road, Tel. 01736-362207, e-mail: pztic@penwith.gov.uk, www.go-cornwall.com. October to Easter Mon–Fri 9am–5pm, in the summer also open Sat and Sun.

Town maps

Available free of charge at the TIC.

Trains

The station is at the lower end of town opposite the bus station. Rail information either at the station itself or on Tel. 0845-7484950, www.nationalrail.co.uk.

Weddings   Penzance offers everything you need for a good wed-
ding, including romantic accommodation, diverse locations for the event, suitable florists and stretch-limo
hire. Information at the *Register Office* in Penzance, Tel.
01736-330093.

When   There's not really a 'best time' to visit West Cornwall, as
to come it depends what is important to the individual.
The climate is influenced by the Gulf Stream, which
gives rise to a long summer and a mild winter, though
the Atlantic creates moderate heat and regular rainfall
equally distributed throughout the year – hence the
deep green of the landscape. In the summer months
the rainfall is usually only brief, and the weather can
change by the minute, but in the winter it can rain for
days (January comes top of the league with 19 days of
rain). In April/May everything is in bloom, so this is the
best time for garden-lovers to come.
Penzance remains relatively quiet until the Golowan Festival at the end of June – at least compared with July/
August, when British and continental tourists storm the
town. September is calmer again and it enjoys the same
average temperatures as June (approx. 17°C), the differ-
ence being that the sea warms up during the summer –
though 'warm up' is to be taken with a pinch of salt!

INDEX

A

Abbey Hotel 15
Abbey Restaurant 15, 22
Acorn Arts Centre **37**, 67, 69, 81
Addicoat, Ian. 40
Admiral Benbow 45, **79**
Alexandra Road 15
Ancient sites 95f
Archie Browns 28
Art Shop, The. 57
Arts Club **38**, 64, 67, 78, 80f

B

Baba, The. 19
Badcocks Gallery. **55f**, 106
Bakehouse 23, **26**, 61
Baker, Denys Val 55
Baker, Martin Val. 40, **53ff**, 56
Barbara Hepworth Museum 58
Barn Club. 82
Bath Inn 19
Battery Rocks 46
Bay, The 23
BBC Radio Cornwall 73
Birch, "Lamorna". 49, **50**
Birch, Lionel 50
Blue Dolphin Backpackers, The . . 17, **18f**
Blue Snappa 78, **80**
Boatshed 24f
Bone Valley Park 20
Books Plus 60
Bopdoq .29
Bosun's Locker 24, 80
Bowen, Phil. 64
Branwell House 51, **64**
Branwell, Maria 64
Breakfast. 30, 80
Brittain, Sarah 53
Brontë, Charlotte, Emily und Anne . . .64
Burley, W.J.. . . . . 60, **62**

C

Cade, Rowena 36
Café Frug. 38
Camilla House 16
Cape Cornwall 17, 92
Captain's Fish Bar 31
Carbis Bay Beach. 91
Cargo. 77
Carn-du .94
Carter, Clive 63
Castle Horneck Youth Hostel 18
Chapel of St Anthony 46
Chapel Street. 41, 44f
Chiverton House 15
Church concerts 68
Cinema magazine 69
Clarke, Joseph 55
Classic Cottages 21
Club 2K. 81
Cocos. **24**, 61, 78
Cornish cream tea 27f
Cornish pasty. **31ff**, 83
Cornish Traditional Cottages. 21
Cornish World 73
Cornishman, The **73f**, 80
Cornwall Contemporary 53
Cornwall Seaside Holiday Cottages . . .21
Cornwall Today. 73
Cornwall Tourist Board. 13
Cove, The. 109
Craig, Linda und Ben. 110
Cross, Tom 63
Crown Inn 80
Cutty Sark Bar 103
Cycle Centre 98

We need you!

Things are always in flux in Penzance and the vicinity – as indeed everywhere – and we would be grateful for any information. Have prices (dramatically) increased, does a restaurant no longer exist, or is a once good hotel suddenly bad? Any feedback, comments, suggestions and criticisms will be most welcome.

We would also like to know about your favourite places, walks, trips, B&Bs, shops etc.

Many thanks!

goldfinch *books*
Muehlendamm 53
22087 Hamburg
Germany   talk2us@goldfinchbooks.de

Name and address: